27
DELUSIONS
OF MANKIND

RICHARD ANDREW KING

Library of Congress Cataloging-in-Publication Data
King, Richard Andrew
27 Delusions of Mankind
ISBN: 978-0-931872-29-7; Price 9000
Date of Publication: 31 August 2021

© **by Richard Andrew King**
Published by Richard King Publications
PO Box 3621
Laguna Hills, CA 92654
(www.RichardKing.net)

ACKNOWLEDGEMENTS

A special thanks to Liana Moisescu
for her beautiful and artistic book
cover and interior design talents.
https://99designs.com/profiles/1544664

CONTACT

Richard Andrew King
PO Box 3621, Laguna Hills, CA 92654-3621
RichardKing.net | Rich@RichardKing.net

TABLE OF CONTENTS

AUTHOR'S INTRODUCTION

The path which the world traverses,
that path I keep at a distance.
Everyone is lost in the world of delusion.
~ Saint Namdev, 13th Century

One mistakes this miserable world for the glitter of gold.
How else to describe this glamorous delusion?
~Saint Ravidas, 15th/16th Century

The whole world is overpowered by delusion.
The delusion is overpowered by none.
~Saint Dariya of Bihar, 17th/18th Century

People are themselves deluded and they
cause delusion to others.
~Saint Dariya

Delusions are false beliefs held to be true. By subscribing to them we become more ignorant and blind to Reality than we already are. How can we be enlightened living in a cave devoid of light? We can't. That's why it is imperative for us to dissolve the delusions that entrap us, enslave us—

from cradle to grave—in a prison of ignorance, keeping us from being free and whole.

This may seem a harsh truth but Truth it is, as difficult as it may be to accept. Saints, from their supernally elevated position, understand this, which is why they take the time through their writings to share this reality with the world to help it become "undeluded," allowing those individuals who desire enlightenment to seek it, acquire it, radiate it.

Saint Namdev queried:

What shall I do? The world sees and yet is blind.

Kabir, a Saint of the 15th/16th Centuries, noted:

The world is blind, engulfed in utter darkness, but to whom can I explain this?

Swami Ji Maharaj, a Saint of the 19th Century, said:

This world is engulfed in the darkness of ignorance.

Saint Jagat Singh of the 20th Century remarked:

There is nothing but utter darkness and misery in this world. It is, indeed, a place where the blind are leading the blind.

Delusions are a major ingredient of this darkness. The sooner we dissolve the delusions which entrap us, the sooner we will live in the Light. This work comments on only 27 Delusions which plague mankind. There are more but for now, twenty seven is a good start.

One final note. For those who deceive and delude others, they would be wise to heed the following warning from Saint Ravidas:

God is not pleased with one who practices deceits.

So . . . here's to the dissolution of delusions and a major step upward from darkness into Divine Light. God Speed!

Richard Andrew King

DELUSION #1

THERE IS NO GOD

I t is hard to fathom why God would not make Himself known to some people, but to some people He has not and that is for Him to know and Him alone. He is the Creator of all that exists, even of those who have no realization of Him.

For individuals who believe there is no God, just take a look at the following quotes from, arguably, the greatest scientist of all time, Sir Isaac Newton:

A Heavenly Master governs all the world as Sovereign of the universe.

This most beautiful system [The Universe] could only proceed from the dominion of an intelligent and powerful Being.

In the absence of any other proof, the thumb alone would convince me of God's existence.

God created everything by number, weight and measure.

It is the perfection of God's works that they are all done with the greatest simplicity. He is the God of order and not of confusion.

And speaking of atheism, Newton remarked:

Atheism is so senseless and odious to mankind that it never had many professors.

Dr. Albert Einstein, the greatest scientist of the 20th Century observed:

Everyone who is seriously involved in the pursuit of science becomes convinced that a spirit is manifest in the laws of the Universe—a spirit vastly superior to that of man, and one in the face of which we, with our modest powers, must feel humble.

And then there is us—ordinary common folk who believe in God. How many billions of people in a multitude of religions understand the existence of a Divine Being? Most of us. It's common sense. We didn't create ourselves. Some Power beyond our understanding created us.

And then there are sacred divine books proclaiming the reality of a Divine Hierarchy, among which are the Holy Bible (Christianity-largest religion in the world), the Quran (Islam-second largest world religion), Vedas (Hinduism), Torah (Judaism) and the Guru Granth Sahib (Sikhism), to name a few.

"But," says John Doe, "I don't believe in God at all and I don't believe in religion." That's fine. Everyone is welcome to their beliefs but let's remember that beliefs are not facts; they're just thoughts, opinions. Beliefs prove nothing; they are inert, powerless, impotent.

For those who doubt the reality of God but who require empirical proof, simply study the King's Numerology™ system and its canon of books. Numerology is the science of numeric coding defining and describing one's life, relationships and destiny. With just a little study, one soon realizes there exists an undeniable correlation between one's numbers (based on the full birth name and birth date) and the circumstances, conditions and events of his/her life. One also comes to realize there is a Power, an Intelligence so vast, so Perfect, that it is beyond the comprehension of the human mind. That Power is what we call God—a living, conscious, ubiquitous energy, universal in scope, omnipotent, omniscient, omnipresent, pervading the entirety of all that is.

The bottom line in proving the existence of God ultimately rests in the personal experiences of each individual rather than in a belief system. God is not, as some people would suggest, a creation of man's mind, at least to this author and billions of other souls worldwide, all of whom, no doubt, understand that God is real and to suggest there is no God is simply naïve, uninformed and, of course . . . a delusion.

DELUSION #2

YOU ONLY LIVE ONCE (Y.O.L.O.)

One of the most treacherous of delusions is "Y.O.L.O.," the acronym for *You Only Live Once*. When we study the writings of Saints of the highest order, we learn that we have had many lives in many forms, that reincarnation and transmigration are structural aspects of the architectural design of this creation.

Reincarnation means to take another body, another form. It doesn't specify a human form but, rather, any living form from the animal, bird, fish, insect or plant kingdoms.

Transmigration is the movement of the soul through the various kingdoms mentioned above. The following explanation of the principle of transmigration is from *Karma—The Definitive Guide to the Supreme Law of this World* (RichardKing.net/books & Amazon.com).

THE WHEEL OF TRANSMIGRATION

All Saints believe in the reality of Transmigration—the movement/ migration of the soul via reincarnation (rebirth in a new body) through various living forms from vegetation to insect to ocean life to birds to animals to human. Transmigration is actually a condemnation of dying and being reborn over and over again in various bodily forms, not necessarily human, until or unless we can ascend into higher planes of existence and exit this lower dimension.

Transmigration is often associated with Indian religions such as Hinduism, Sikhism, Buddhism and Jainism. However, great thinkers such as Socrates, Plato and Pythagoras also believed in transmigration. As its truth is realized, Western cultures will follow suit as the deeper secrets of spirituality expand.

There is a belief that transmigration and reincarnation are New Age concepts. Actually, they're not. They're ages old. Pythagoras, for example, died approximately 495 years BCE (Before the Common Era). Socrates died in 399 BCE; Plato died approximately 417 BCE. These were three of the greatest thinkers in history and they lived well over 2,300 years ago. Verily, one could make the argument that Western understanding of spirituality is late to the party.

The process of transmigration is often referred to as the Wheel or Cycle of Transmigration, also known as The Wheel of Eighty-Four, Eighty-Four Lakhs, Chaurasi or simply "Wheel" for short. One lakh equals 100,000 units.

The Wheel of Transmigration is a construct of 8,400,000 forms of life into which the soul can incarnate. And here's the critical point: of this 8,400,000 forms of life, the highest form is man, and only man has the ability to know of God and merge his soul into the ocean of God's energy. This means that 8,399,999 other forms of life are left devoid of divine access. Only man has the privilege of being God-conscious. This is why the human body is sacred beyond belief and is referred to by Saints as the Top of Creation. Only in the human body can one know there's a God and even merge himself with God. How special it is to be human!

As the famous Indian Saint, Guru Nanak, states: (*Guru Nanak, His Mystic Teachings*, Professor J. R. Puri, Radha Soami Satsang Beas, 1982, 2nd Edition, p.283)

> *Precious is the human birth; only the saints know its worth.*

And: (Ibid., p.341)

> *Men are victims of their evil passions and are dominated by their worldly attachments. They forget that the human birth is a very rare gift, the only one in eighty-four lakhs of species for attaining release from birth and death.*

Nanak goes on to say: (Ibid., p.50)

> *Not only does God live within the human body, but it is only within this body that He manifests himself. Thus, it is doubly blessed.*

From the Bible we read: (I Corinthians 3:16)

> *Know ye not that ye are the temple of God and that the Spirit of God dwelleth in you? If any man defile the temple of God, him shall God destroy, for the temple of God is holy, which temple ye are.*

If one is not convinced about the importance of the human body within the Wheel of Transmigration, the following quote from Saint Charan Singh should make one think deeply about the extreme and incredible gift each of us has been given. (*Quest for Light*, p.166)

The human body is not given to us in every birth. We get it only after millions of lives, and it is a very rare and precious gift not to be wasted upon the perishable things and objects of this world.

Millions of lives! We have been given this unbelievable gift of the human body—the Crown Jewel of all living forms in this creation—after eons of time enslaved in the Wheel of Transmigration in the other 8,399,999 forms of life! If this does not put things in perspective as to how utterly blessed we are as human beings, then what will?

How many of us take our temporal human body for granted, not knowing the immensity of goodness and opportunity it affords? And since human life is temporal, would it not be wise to make the most of its use while we can? Of course it would be, and we'd better, lest upon our death we are thrown back into the Wheel of Eighty-Four, for God only knows how long. Contemplatingly, how many eons of time comprise 8,400,000 lives? We don't know, but let's hope we adopt the spiritual program of elevating our consciousness so we continue making upward progress on the Ladder of Life, thus avoiding the Wheel of Eighty Four and its unthinkable enslavement.

In consideration, Saint Jagat Singh offers the following warning which helps place this entire discussion of the Wheel of Transmigration in its proper perspective. (*The Science of the Soul*, p.38)

(Unfortunately), the true value of the human body is realized after death when man regrets that he has squandered his most precious possession. The result is that he has to go to hell or to lower births.

In his book, *The Dawn of Light*, Maharaj Sawan Singh comments: (Radha Soami Satsang Beas, Punjab, India, 1st edition, 1985, p.192)

In the cycle of transmigration, birth as a human being takes a long time to come again. Once the opportunity is lost, there is the cycle to go through. A slip from the top of a mountain means a heavy fall, and a stop on the way down is rare.

Guru Nanak weighs in: (*Philosophy of the Masters*, Vol. 1, Huzur Maharaj Sawan Singh, Radha Soami Satsang Beas, Punjab, India, p.30)

The cycle of transmigration is dreadful, and it is beyond the comprehension of the human intellect.

Swami Ji Maharaj, the Great Saint of Agra (19th Century), corroborates Saint Charan Singh's statement regarding transmigration: (*The Science of the Soul*, p.64)

This valuable body you got after roaming in millions of lower lives. Now do not lose it in vain pursuits. Take heed! Give your attention to Devotion. Have pity on your poor soul and save it from transmigration's wheel.

In capitalizing the word *Devotion* he is referencing the worship of God, adherence to Divine Laws, as well as the purification and perfection of our being.

Swami Ji Maharaj offers this dire and very sobering warning in his book *Sar Bachan: Book 2, Sayings*: (#86)

If, however, you don't believe in either what I say or in the writings of the Saints, the path of Transmigration lies before you. Walk upon it by all means.

[end excerpt]

To conclude this, Saint Sawan Singh states in his book *Spiritual Gems*:

> *The principle of reincarnation is a fact. It is part of the Creator's scheme.*

So here's the danger with the Y.O.L.O. delusion. If we buy into it, that "you only live once," not only will we be in direct contrast to the Saint's declaration that reincarnation and transmigration are a fact of life, but also that we might do many things in this life that we would not do if we knew such behaviors would deny us a future human birth. In other words, we could be forced to live in sub-human lives for millions of years—all because we accepted the Y.O.L.O. delusion of only living once. Well, we may only live once in a human form. However, we won't escape life in the Wheel of Transmigration and its framework of 8,399,999 lower forms of life.

You only live once, aka Y.O.L.O., is not only a delusion, it is a fraud designed to entrap souls and bind them to this nether world. Unless you want to remain in this world, don't subscribe to it. Let it dissolve into the ocean of delusion where it belongs.

DELUSION #3

WE HAVE TOTAL FREE WILL

Having "total free will" is one of the greatest delusions of mankind. We think we have free will but we do not. The spiritual truth is that our lives are destined to the breath and that destiny was created before we were born.

Dr. Albert Einstein, the most famous scientist of the 20th Century, Nobel Laureate for Physics in 1921, and Time magazine's Person of the 20th Century proclaims quite beautifully and poetically:

Everything is determined, the beginning as well as the end, by forces over which we have no control. It is determined for the insect, as well as for the star. Human beings, vegetables or cosmic dust—we all dance to a mysterious tune, intoned in the distance by an invisible piper.

If "everything is determined," how can we have free will?

The following quotes by Sawan Singh, a 19th/20th Century Saint, are from his classic book, *Spiritual Gems*.

Before a person is born, his entire life or destiny is settled.

And . . .

The total number of breaths which one is to take till death, the morsels which one is to eat and the steps which one is to walk are all preordained at birth and no one can alter, decrease or increase them.

And . . .

What destiny has planned for you will come to pass without any planning on your part. Your destiny will cause you to act and make effort according to its plan.

And . . .

Old age, health, poverty, richness, sickness, disease, wealth, learning, honor, dishonor and time of death are all pre-ordained while a man is in the womb of his mother, so a wise man never worries or frets or regrets anything.

And . . .

And, again, our present life is already determined before we are born.

In *Philosophy of the Masters*, Volume 1, Sawan Singh remarks:

> *We are powerless to change our destiny. Whatever is destined in our fate must happen.*

And . . .

> *There is an account of every minute of a man's life. Illness, poverty, health, wealth and so on are all predestined . . . Whatever is happening is all preordained.*

In *Dawn of Light*, Sawan Singh says:

> *Take for granted that all that has happened, is happening or will happen, is with His will.*

This message of a preordained life is taught by all Saints of the highest order. It is designed to liberate souls from the delusion of total free will and set them on a path of Truth. Saints, however, are not the only ones who profess this principle of preordination. From Ecclesiastes 3:1 in the *Holy Bible* is this very clear statement:

> *To every thing there is a season, and a time to every purpose under the heaven.*

If everything has a season, a time and a purpose, how can we have free will?

In St. Matthew 10:30 from the *Bible* we read:

> *The very hairs of your head are all numbered.*

Stop and think for a moment about the depth, magnitude and profundity of this statement—that every one of the hairs on our head is numbered. Does that sound like the number of hairs on our head is a random occurrence, an accident? Since the hairs on our head are all numbered, as the *Bible* states, it can't be an accident. It has to be preordained, predetermined by design. Furthermore, what does this say about the other aspects of our life such as *illness, poverty, health, wealth and so on* as already stated by Saint Sawan Singh?

The *Quran* makes this statement:

> *What God writes on your forehead you will become.*

The *Granth Sahib* offers this comment:

> *The Unknowable Lord's pen inscribes the Destinies of all beings on their foreheads.*

A Yiddish proverb declares:

> *If a man is destined to drown, he will drown even in a spoonful of water.*

A French proverb joins in:

> *He that is born to be hanged shall never be drowned.*

The great writer of The Iliad, Homer, affirms:

> *No living man can send me to the shades before my time; no man of woman born, coward or brave, can shun his destiny.*

Benjamin Disraeli, Prime Minister of Great Britain from 1804 to 1881 observes:

> *A consistent soul believes in destiny, a capricious one in chance.*

Guru Amardas, the 3rd of the Ten Sikh Gurus, asserts:

> *God himself forces his creatures into destined paths of karmas (fruits of previous actions) over which they have no control and which cannot be effaced. Whatever is destined to take place must take place.*

If *whatever is destined to take place must take place*, how can we change the course of our life? Obviously, we can't, which underscores the reality that we do not have total free will and to think and profess that we do is to cling to the great delusion that we have total free will.

To pacify some souls who declare that we have free will, Saint Charan Singh has noted that if we have any free will at all it is in how we react to the conditions and events of our life, thus generating a limited free will. Yet, he ultimately proclaims we have no free will at all, just like all Saints, Mystics and evolved souls have declared. He states in his book *Quest for Light*:

> *All men come into this world with a destiny of their own which goes on pushing them relentlessly on the course already marked out for them. Man is completely helpless. Why then worry?*

And in another supporting quote he remarks:

> *Nothing can happen which is not in your destiny.*

These quotes from other individuals could go on forever and ever. They are endless among those who understand the Divine Architecture of this creation.

Individuals who doubt this reality, once again are enjoined to study the King's Numerology^{tm}. When we actually see the relationship between our life and our numbers, the truth eventually registers in our heads. We are inextricably bound to a destiny that has been predesigned and predetermined for each of us. Verily, the concept of total free will is, indeed, a great delusion, and when we dissolve this delusion we move one step closer to the Light, manifesting a Divine, not human, Reality.

DELUSION #4

I'M A VICTIM

No one is a victim in this world unless it is a victim of their own making. Victimhood is one of the greatest and most insidious of all delusions. It smacks in the face of Karmic Law—the immutable, inviolable, unavoidable law of this creation.

Guru Nanak, a great Saint of the 15th/16th Century, stated:

I blame not another. I blame my own karmas. Whatever I sowed, so did I reap. Why then put the blame on others?

In other words, Nanak is taking full responsibility for his own actions. He is saying he is no victim and cannot blame anyone else but himself for what happens to him. Why? Because the supreme Law of this world is Karma. We sow, we reap and we cannot reap what we do not sow. What we put onto the circle of life, circles back to encircle us eventually. We simply cannot escape the reactions of our actions and to think otherwise and blame others for what happens to us, while proclaiming ourselves a victim, is an absolute and insidious delusion.

The problem is that our karmas are not necessarily instant. They may take years, decades, even lifetimes to circle back to us but circle back they will. Of this there is no doubt. Whether our actions were good or bad, positive or negative, ethical or unethical, truthful or untruthful, loving or hateful, eventually they all come home to roost and "home" is us.

The following excerpts are from *Karma—The Definitive Guide to the Supreme Law of this World*, Chapter 9 "Karma of Victimhood." (RichardKing.net/books & Amazon.com)

[Excerpt 1]
Being a victim is one of the outstanding delusions of this world. We can't blame anyone for feeling like a victim because they may not understand the connection between this life and its actions and past lives and their actions. If we could see our past lives, we would absolutely know we're never a victim, but such vision only occurs as we climb higher on the Divine Ladder of Consciousness.

[Excerpt 2]
Not seeing ourselves as a victim when we are injured, or beset with some challenging situation, is often difficult because Karmic Law and reincarnation are not considered basic principles of life for most of humanity. Yet, Saints inform us that reincarnation and karma are integral aspects of this world's spiritual architecture. Therefore, we can either accept this reality and work with it or ignore it and attempt to live in denial, which will not help us grow spiritually or remain balanced and centered.

Some people may believe that if they perform actions in secret they will escape the consequences. Not so. Saint Sawan Singh states: (Philosophy of the Masters, Vol. 1, p.22)

One cannot escape the result of one's actions by performing them in secret. The consequences of such actions have to be borne sometime or the other. It is therefore clear that whatever weal or woe, joy or sorrow we experience, it is all due to our own actions, and we should not blame anyone else for it.

[Excerpt 3]
Are we really an innocent victim in anything? Karma says, "No. We sowed, we reaped, we weeped, we became a victim by our own doing, not someone else's."

This brings us to the point of recompense—the karmic time to pay up. Accidents, tragedies, hardships, etc., are nothing more than Karmic Law in action—the repaying of karmic debts from previous lives now seeking retribution.

Thus, it's not God's fault for what we experience in life; it's our fault. We must remember, God doesn't prevent us from making choices; nor does He prevent us from experiencing the consequences of those choices. When we kill, we must be killed—sooner or later. When we play the part of the killer, we eventually must play the part of the victim, and when we are the victim, it is no one else's fault but our own. The same thing goes for all the untoward things we've done in the past. We could not be the victim unless we had created victims through our own negative and nefarious actions.

Therefore, because of karma, there simply are no accidents in this world. What we think is an accident is nothing more than karmic reconciliation.

[Excerpt 4]

From *The King's Book of Numerology, Volume 1 – Foundations & Fundamentals*, page 73, we read:

> *Perfect Master Maharaj Charan Singh Ji says, "There are no innocent victims" in this dimension. We all reap exactly what we have sown and there is no escaping this fact. It is Law in this creation. If we plant seeds of fire, we will reap seeds of fire. If we plant seeds of sorrow, we will reap seeds of sorrow. Likewise, if we plant seeds of love, harmony, purity, balance, generosity, honesty, honor and right behavior, we will reap their fruit. In essence, we generate the vehicles of our own purification. We are the sculptors of our own destiny, our own pain, our own suffering, our own cleansing.*

What else is there to say? We sow, we reap; we cannot reap what we do not sow. This is the law of this world and it explains why no one is a victim in this world. Victimhood is yet another powerful delusion that entraps us and keeps us from being mature and free.

*There are no innocent
victims in this dimension.
We all reap exactly
what we have sown.*

~ Saint Charan Singh

DELUSION #5

LIFE IS UNFAIR AND UNJUST

J ust as there is no victim in this world, there is also nothing that is unfair and unjust. Once again, the reason is Karma and its never ceasing cycling reality of cause and effect.

Says Saint Ravidas: (15th/16th Century)

Whatever you have sown the same you shall reap. No change in it shall there ever be.

Saint Dariya of Bihar (17th/18th Century) remarks:

The sower of the poison cannot but be engulfed in the poison.

Saint Dadu Dayal (16th Century) declares:

What you have not done will never befall you. Only what you have done will befall you.

And . . .

What has been done before appears now; what is done now will appear hereafter.

And . . .

As one doeth through thought, word and deed, so doth one receive as fruit.

And . . .

Knowingly does the person perform good or bad deeds. Knowingly does he leap into the fire. Let no one blame God.

And . . .

Whatever beings thou killest, the same ones will kill thee in turn. Whatever beings thou savest, the same ones will save thee in return.

From the Bible, Galatians 6:7, comes this truth:

Be not deceived; God is not mocked: for whatsoever a man soweth, that shall he also reap.

The message from Saint after Saint, era after era, time after time is always the same, Karma—the Law of sowing and reaping—is the basis for all our blessings and curses, weals and woes, unfair lives and fair lives; unjust lives and just lives.

How long will it take humanity to grasp this simple reality which has been since the world became? It is *the* architecture of this creation, like it or not.

Those who go through life constantly complaining that life is unjust are themselves the actual cause of their plight. Those who feel their life is just, created it in previous lives and incarnations.

The truth is that life is totally fair and just. Karma guarantees it. As Saint Charan Singh declares:

Karma will take care of our choice automatically.

Karma will also take care of the circumstances of our life automatically. Spiritual maturity dictates that we rise to the level of this truth and quit complaining about the very nature of our life if we feel it is unjust, for it is so because we created its "unjust" reality and are now having to live what we created.

How sad it is for some people and factions of humanity to keep wailing, moaning and groaning about the injustice they perceive in the world, especially those injustices they feel are directed to them, when they were the ones who actually created them? When will they grow into the expanded consciousness that they are the ones who created everything they're experiencing? Unbeknownst to them, they are simply adding kerosene to the fire of their own predicament and making it harder for them to break the chains of their own delusions.

As we compile these issues of unjustness, unfairness and victimhood together, we see the insidious nature of their delusions and how such delusions generate greater and greater degrees of darkness in a world already consumed with not only darkness but blindness as well. We can't heal the blindness of others, but we can heal our own blindness by living in the Light of Karmic Law, knowing that what we sow we will eventually reap and to this end never blame others for our own actions because life really is fair and just and to think otherwise is a pure delusion.

DELUSION #6

UTOPIAN IDEOLOGY
OF EQUALITY

The Utopian ideology that everyone is equal on this earth or should be equal is yet another misguided sentiment and dark delusion. The very thing that separates every human being on the planet is our inherent inequality, not our equality.

Yes, we're all equal in the eyes of God in the sense that we're all human but that's as far as the truth extends. Each of us possesses our own destiny and our destinies are all different, created by Divine Design, so how can we all be equal, as some people want to believe? We simply can't. It's impossible.

As we all know, there are people who are driven to succeed in life, and there are those who prefer to lay around, do nothing and expect others to take care of them—feed them, clothe them, house them. How is this equal, and how can a society be considered equal when such obvious differences exist? It's ludicrous. Such a Utopian Society is a product of wishful thinking, not rational thinking.

Honestly, how much equality actually prevails in any culture on the planet? In the military there are multiple ranks of achievement. Is a Private First Class equal to a General? Is a common athlete equal to an Olympic Gold Medalist? Is a successful business person equal to a vagabond?

Obviously, every person deserves respect as a human being but personal traits of intelligence, ambition, drive, honesty, ethics, morals, talents, sensitivities, caring, nurturing, supporting, common sense, well-being, etc., are all different in different people. How is it possible for a society to be equal when such diversity defines us?

Then there are parents who love and care for their children and do all they can to help them succeed in life. Such souls are in contrast to parents who could care less about their children's well-being or success in life? How are they equal?

From a spiritual point of reference, there are souls on the planet who are highly advanced and close to making a transition to a higher realm. Simultaneously, there are also souls on the planet who are just coming into the human form for the first time from the lower species. How can such souls be considered equal?

And what of those souls who choose to violate societal laws and mores in comparison to those who live by societal laws? They're obviously not equal, so why should they be considered as equals and having equal rights?

These contrasts could go on forever, but they've made their point. Creating a Utopian Society in this world is nothing more than wishful thinking combined with delusions of grandeur. In short, the Utopian Ideology of Equality is simply a delusion. Nothing more. It has no substance and certainly no future.

Once again, studying the King's Numerology™ will make it crystal clear that a Utopian Ideology of Equality is impossible to achieve. Every human being's numerology chart contains multiple energies defined by numbers and letters. No two numerology charts are the same; many are in direct contrast to other charts, to other people. Given this fact, there could never be equality among people.

For example, let's say one person has a Lifepath of 4 (determined by the day, month and year of birth) and another individual has a 5 Lifepath. The Lifepath reveals the actual path in life a person is to follow. It's basically the script of a person's life, just like an actor/actress who reads a script.

In this example, the numbers 4 and 5 are diametrically opposed, i.e., they're opposites. The 4 Lifepath is focused on stability, roots, structure, security, convention, tradition, work and service. The 5 Lifepath is one of freedom, flight, change, detachment, movement, motion, versatility, non-convention and non-tradition. The 4 is an earth sign; the 5 is a fire sign. Earth and fire don't blend well, to say the least. Therefore, how will these two individuals get along? Remember, the 4 and 5 are opposites, so the chances of them creating a warm and fuzzy relationship and sharing the same ideology will be challenging, to say the least.

This example of the 4 Lifepath versus the 5 Lifepath represents just one aspect of a person's destiny. There are many aspects to a numerology chart. Some generate resonance; some dissonance. The reality is that even two people may not be able to create a Utopian status between them because of their numeric differences, not to mention the 8,000,000,000 (eight billion) people living on planet earth as registered in the world population clock. (www.worldometers.info/world-population)

Take another example—a 1 Lifepath versus a 2 Lifepath. Like the 4-5 opposition, the 1 and 2 are also opposites. The 1 Lifepath involves lessons of the self, personal identity, individuality, independence, initiation, action, activation, reason, leadership, genesis, and all things yang and male. The 1 is a fire sign—hot and active.

The 2 Lifepath addresses lessons of relationship and others, not the self; of partnership not leadership; dependence, not independence; emotion, not reason; indirect action rather than direct action; support, caring, helping and all things yin and female. The 2 is a water sign and seeks to be the power behind the throne, not the one sitting on the throne.

Another example. Contrast the 7 Lifepath with an 8 Lifepath. The 7 seeks solitude and internalization; the 8 seeks social interaction and externalization. The 7 is introverted while the 8 is extroverted. The 7 is studious, inquisitive, withdrawing; the 8 is engaging, interactive and connective. The 7 has no desire to be socially involved; the 8 craves social involvement. The 7 is an air sign; the 8 is an earth sign. There is no Utopia here, for sure.

In no way can this triumvirate of the numeric oppositions of the 1 vs. 2, 4 vs. 5, and 7 vs. 8 be considered equal because they are obviously not equal in attributes or characteristics. Each number and its energies are very different from the other numbers and their energies. It is how this world was created and to think that there can be a Utopian society where everyone is equal to everyone else is simply myopic, to say the very least.

Saints tell us that this world, in fact, can never be a paradise, a Utopia, or even a heaven.

Saint Charan Singh declares:

There can never be a paradise on this earth.

And . . .

In this world there is nothing but strife, struggle and conflict. Lasting peace can never be found within the domain of the mind and senses. So it was from the time of creation and so it will always be.

And . . .

> *This world will never improve . . . We cannot reform this world, and*
> *this world will never become a heaven but will remain at daggers*
> *drawn, and there always will be killing in this world. Saints do not*
> *come to reform this world. They just come to take us away from this*
> *world.*

Christ stated: (Matthew 10:34)

> *Think not that I am come to bring peace on earth. I came not to*
> *send peace but a sword.*

Why the sword? Answer: to separate souls from this most wicked world, just as Saint Charan Singh stated, *They [Saints) just come to take us away from this world.*

So how do Saints and Mystics define this world? Saint Sawan Singh has a simple explanation.

> *The world is a furnace in whose fires the soul is purified.*

Obviously, Saints do not think much of this world. The simple truth— the Utopian Ideology of Equality that is espoused by some individuals is nothing more than a grand delusion. Pay it no mind, for the idea itself is mindless.

DELUSION #7

LIFE IS A RANDOM HAPPENING

With all the craziness going on in the world, one would think, and rightly so, that there is no rhyme or reason to life, that everything that occurs is indiscriminate, arbitrary, accidental—that life is, indeed, a random happening.

From our extremely myopic human viewpoint, this is understandable. However, from the elevated perspective of Saints it's just the reverse. There is a Divine Order to everything that exists whether we're aware of it or not.

Saint Sawan Singh states:

> *Take for granted that all that has happened, is happening or will happen, is with His will.*

Underscore "take for granted."

Saint Charan Singh remarks with a comfortable note:

> *Everything is happening as the Lord wants it to happen. Not a leaf can stir without His command.*

Talk about moving from "random" to "specificity" in two short sentences! Obviously, our human point of view is a little off the mark, to be kind. But we're "down here" looking up while Saints are "up there" looking down. "There" is far beyond our vision and level of consciousness, which is why Saints come to the world—to inform and teach us of higher Truths, higher planes of existence, higher realms of being, or as Christ would say, "In my Father's house are many mansions: if it were not so, I would have told you." (John 14:2)

Joining the "specificity" discussion, Saint Sawan Singh says:

> *There is an account of every minute of a man's life.*

Stop and think about this for a moment, or maybe even a day—that every sixty seconds of every human being's life has already been accounted for. How much more specific can our human lives be? "Random" does not exist in this paradigm.

Guru Nanak submits this statement:

> *Whatever pleases the Lord comes to pass for nothing is in the hands of mortal men.*

How declarative is this, that "nothing is in the hands of mortal men!" What does this say about the diminutive status of human beings and their impotence? Obviously, we mortals have a lot of growing up and maturing to do.

Saint Charan Singh continues the discussion:

> *Whatever has to happen must happen and what is not destined to happen will never take place. Nothing can happen which is not in your destiny. We are all reaping what we have sown in the past. Each individual has his own karma to face and this destiny cannot be changed . . . Our entire life—in the minutest details—is already marked out even before we are born.*

Unpack this paragraph! There is at least a month of thought and meditation to engage in.

1. *Whatever has to happen must happen.*

2. *What is not destined to happen will never take place.*

3. *Nothing can happen which is not in your destiny.*

4. *We are all reaping what we have sown in the past.*

5. *Each individual has his own karma to face.*

6. *This destiny cannot be changed.*

7. *Our entire life in the minutest details is already marked out*

8. *Even before we are born.*

This amalgam of Divine Truth puts to rest the delusion that life is a random happening. It's not, and the previous quotes clearly put the "random happening" delusion to sleep, forever.

DELUSION #8

WE CAN CHANGE
THE WORLD

This delusion can be nullified quickly. As Saint Charan Singh states:

> *This world will never improve . . . We cannot reform this world, and this world will never become a heaven but will remain at daggers drawn, and there always will be killing in this world. Saints do not come to reform this world. They just come to take us away from this world.*

One of the major ingredients missing in the human mindset—most likely because of its ignorance and arrogance— is the reality that this world has already been Divinely Designed and cannot be changed or reformed, in spite of man's endless and ubiquitous monologue that man can "change the world."

The first statement in the above quote is, *This world will never improve.* What more needs to be said? Why go through life under the delusion that we humans can improve the world? How void is this statement of Divinity,

Spirituality, God? It is not only an arrogant statement, it is ignorant and reckless and totally bereft of any thought that a Higher Power exists other than man.

Even if man could change the world, what would he change it to? You'll notice that whenever someone talks about changing the world he or she never says to what, change to what? Just uttering the thought of change says nothing. It's empty jargon. It needs clarification.

This world is 4.5 billion years old. It is basically a rock composed of tectonic plates that are constantly changing and causing massive changes in its outer structure. The world's climate is always changing, too, and has never stopped changing. It is doing what it's going to do and man is not going to change its natural life. He may destroy it (the world). He may be destroyed by it. However, the idea of a changing earth, a changing environment, is nothing new. The world is 4.5 billion years old after all— 4.5 billion years of relentless change and transformation. If we desire to change anything, we should focus on changing ourselves and purifying our own consciousness.

Saint Charan Singh states that the world will never improve because it has been created by Divine Design. It has a purpose.

Saint Sawan Singh remarks:

The world is a furnace in whose fires the soul is purified.

This statement explains why the world exists. It exists to purify the soul of each of us so we have the opportunity to rise higher into Realms of Divinity. The world is basically a proving ground for the soul. It has purpose. It has design, but that design cannot be changed, so to talk about changing the world is unnecessary.

In Charan Singh's quote above he says, "We cannot reform this world" and "Saints do not come to reform this world." We can't reform this world and Saints can't reform it because it has already been designed and architected by God. It can't be reformed, recreated, redesigned or restructured. It can't also be changed. Therefore, "Changing the World" is an empty idea and yet another delusion in the pantheon of human ignorance.

This world will never improve.
We cannot reform this world.

~ Saint Charan Singh

The world is a furnace in whose fires the soul is purified.

~ Saint Sawan Singh

DELUSION #9

THERE CAN
BE PEACE ON EARTH

This is a wonderful thought—to have peace on earth. Yet it is a delusion. Peace exists in higher realms of Light. It does not exist here in this God-forsaken world, not because God has forsaken the world but because the world has forsaken God.

Says Saint Charan Singh:

> *In this world there is nothing but strife, struggle and conflict. Lasting peace can never be found within the domain of the mind and senses. So it was from the time of creation and so it will always be.*

Peace may exist temporarily from time to time in the world but never forever. After all, "This world is a furnace in whose fires the soul is purified." How can any person find peace when we're all living in a furnace of active fire?

Saint Charan Singh continues:

> *This whole world is a dark and filthy dungeon.*

This doesn't exactly sound like a place of peace and happiness, does it? How can anyone find peace when he is groveling around in the dark and filth? Yuck! It's no different than living in a sewer with its hoard of rats and feculence.

Saint Jagat Singh says:

> *There is nothing but utter darkness and misery in this world. It is indeed a place where the blind are leading the blind.*

Do darkness and misery sound like fun and peace to you?

Saint Sawan Singh notes:

> *This world is the lowest and most miserable of all.*

And quite directly. . .

> *There is no peace in this world.*

Saint Dariya of Bihar (17th/18th Century) says:

> *This world is, indeed, an ocean of miseries . . . a sea of sorrow.*

Saint Tukaram (17th Century) observes:

> *There is no peace on this earth.*

Saint Ravidas exclaims:

> *The world is a house of collyrium (an abode of evil); a veritable well of the poison of egotism.*

And . . .

> *This world is a field of suffering known to all. The wise man reaps his harvest with God's Name while the fool, weeping, reaps it in tears.*

Mira Bai, a female Saint, succinctly comments:

> *This world is truly a cauldron of evil.*

"An ocean of miseries," "an abode of evil," "a veritable well of the poison of egotism," "a field of suffering known to all," and "a cauldron of evil" aren't exactly sentiments of peace and joy, are they?

Saint Charan Singh remarks:

> *Saints do not come into this world to let us live in peace with the world . . . but to detach us from it and take us out of it.*

As Jesus mentions: (Matthew 10: 34)

> *Think not that I am come to send peace on earth; I came not to send peace but a sword.*

The "sword" was a reference to cutting our ties to this dark and foreboding world.

Is it not strange that at Christmas time signs of "Peace on Earth" are displayed everywhere as if that was Christ's message? Nothing could be further from the truth. Christ didn't say that. He said, "I come not to send peace on earth; I came not to send peace but a sword." So why is Christ's message being distorted, even falsified?

Of course, it would be wonderful to have peace on earth but, as we see, no ambassador of Divine Truth says anything of the kind; just the opposite.

Saints and Mystics of the highest order do not live in a wardrobe of hope. They live in the Divine garb of Truth and they teach it without apology, mitigation or resignation. Their goal is to take us Home where there is Oneness with the Divine, where there is harmony, peace, joy, light and love. All these wonderful attributes exist in Higher Realms, but they do not exist here in this very low, dark and miserable world.

This is why Saint Charan Singh states:

> *You do not belong to this world. Just live in the world and get out of it.*

The way we get out of this world is to focus on purifying ourselves, perfecting our virtues, developing our character, being stewards of our divine human form, loving others, seeking all that's healthy, whole and harmonious and answering the Divine Call when that occurs, as it will when God sees fit to make it so.

Think not that I am come
to send peace on earth:
I came not to send peace,
but a sword.

~ Bible: Matthew 10:34

DELUSION #10

PEACE EQUALS PASSIVITY

P eace does not equal passivity. Passivity is an invitation to domination. Thinking that passivity equates to peace is not only erroneous, it is a lethally dangerous delusion, too often promoted by active zealots who are misguided and misinformed about what peace actually is.

The following excerpt—"Peace at Any Price is Not Peace, It's Slavery"—is taken from *The Black Belt Book of Life: Secrets of a Martial Arts Master* (RichardKing.net/books & Amazon.com).

[Excerpt]
Too often, people operate under the premise that peace should be maintained at all costs? All costs? Would you give up your life to an attacker to maintain his peace? If you don't value yourself or your life, then what is your life worth? What are your values worth? If you're a woman and some predator wants to rape you and take away your dignity, health and well-being and you believe that by being passive and allowing him to have his way with you, you will acquire peace, you won't. On a personal note, in my martial arts career I have seen the effects of rape. They're

horrible, often crippling women for the rest of their lives, not to mention the lives of those they love and who love them.

There is an erroneous belief that peace equates to passivity. This is incorrect. Peace is not passivity. Peace is an active state of balance between the opposing polarities of passivity on the one hand and activity on the other.

To understand this, let's use cancer as an example. In one sense, cancer is a passively growing disease. If we equated peace with passivity, then we would say that cancer is a peaceful disease. Nothing could be further from the truth. If cancer gets out of control, violent measures may have to be used to destroy it—chemotherapy, radiation, surgery. These are violent measures but necessary in order to bring the individual back into a state of balance and peace. The moral of the story: peace sometimes demands great and violent action to preserve it, just as if one had to defend his life from someone who wanted to destroy it. If we acquiesce under threat of harm by believing that peace at such a price will bring peace, then our delusion will enslave us and we will deserve exactly what we get . . . slavery, or worse.

All decent people want peace. The rub is that there can never be peace in this world because of its polarized nature of opposites: positive/negative, light/dark, up/down, back/forth, hot/cold, day/night, man/woman, yin/yang, and on and on and on. In a teeter-totter world, struggle is the way of life because we're always fighting to maintain our balance, as well we should, and must to have a fulfilled life.

It is because of the intrinsic nature of this world that 20th Century Master, Charan Singh, admonished people to, *Just live in the creation and get out of it*. Out of it? Yes. Mystic teachings explain that other worlds, other mansions, other realms exist that are beyond the physical plane, which is where we are currently living. To learn more about these mystic teachings, read *Messages from the Masters: Timeless Truths for Spiritual Seekers.* (www.RichardKing.net/books and Amazon.com)

The thing of note in the mundane world is that if we want peace, we must be willing to fight for it. To sell whatever we own, including our freedom and lives, in hopes of creating peace will not work, ever. Peace cannot be created through pacification if someone is bent on taking our life. We must sometimes unfortunately fight to preserve a life of peace because peace at any price is not peace, it is slavery.

[end excerpt]

Living trapped within your self
certainly isn't savory;
Peace at any price is not peace,
it's slavery.

On another personal note, when my United States Air Force fighter pilot father was stationed at George Air Force Base when I was in Elementary School, there was a sign over the main gate to the base that read: *Power For Peace.* As a young lad, I didn't fully understand what that meant until I entered my teen years and began my martial arts career. What I have learned is that power creates peace because when you have power, trouble goes the other way. It is a fact life, and to believe that peace equals passivity is a delusion and a dangerous one because predators are always on the hunt for those souls who cannot or will not defend themselves, even if their health, well-being and life are at stake.

Therefore, to create peace in our lives, we must put to rest the delusion that peace equates to passivity, because it doesn't. Passivity leads to enslavement, or worse.

We must also adopt an aggressive mindset toward those entities who seek to deprive us of our God-given right to life and to its peaceful status. If we're not willing to fight for our own peace, then what right do we have to claim it?

*Peace at any price is not
peace. It is slavery.
and . . .
If we're not willing to fight
for our own peace, then what right
do we have to claim it?*

~ Richard Andrew King

DELUSION #11

PRACTICE MAKES PERFECT

Be thou perfect.
~ Bible - Genesis 17:1

Be ye therefore perfect, even as your Father
which is in Heaven is perfect.
~ Matthew 5:48

Be as perfect as your Creator.
~ Saint Jagat Singh

There is such a thing as perfection and our
purpose for living is to find that perfection
and show it forth.
"Jonathan Livingston Seagull"
~ Richard Bach

How often have we heard the phrase, "Practice Makes Perfect?"

Actually, this is incorrect. *Perfect Practice Makes Perfect.* Practice simply makes a habit. The habit can be good but it can also be bad, but when we learn to practice perfectly, then we realize that "Practice Makes Perfect" is a delusion.

Perfection is our goal as human beings. Why else have a human birth? However, in order to be perfect we have to work at it and practice perfectly. We can't just give lip service to perfection. Doing the same thing over and over again will not necessarily create perfection unless the effort is executed perfectly. Hence the phrase, "Perfect practice makes perfect."

Saint Jagat Singh remarks:

> *God's work is permanent and everlasting and exists in a state of perfection in every man.*

And . . .

> *Man is the top of all creation, the perfect handiwork of Nature in all aspects. He contains within himself the key to unlock the mystery of the Universe and to contact the Creator. It is the greatest and the highest good fortune of any sentient being to be born in the form of man.*

PERFECT PRACTICE

Perfect practice, perfect makes.
Simple practice makes a habit.
If it's perfection we desire,
then we must make *Perfection* habit.

Simple habits, habits make.
The outcome of our loves
becomes extraordinary in the law
that *perfect is as perfect does.*

When we spend time in forming
those things we want in 'grooves'
then we must practice perfectly
for *perfect is as perfect moves.*

We can't expect perfection
from results our effort takes
if we don't practice perfectly,
for *perfect is as perfect makes.*

~ Richard Andrew King

There are souls who believe perfection cannot be achieved. These are souls who have never or may never achieve perfection because their beliefs will restrict them from doing so.

However, as the previous quotes declare, perfection is possible. It just takes dedication, discipline, effort, time, relentless perseverance and the unyielding commitment to the reality that *Perfect Practice Makes Perfect.*

63

DELUSION #12

THINGS HAPPEN COINCIDENTALLY

How many times in life have we heard the following phrase or something like it—"What a coincidence!" This can happen any time, any where, with whomever. We bump into somebody or something happens and we declare, "What a coincidence!"

Actually, there are no coincidences in this world. Everything is by Divine Design. We may not be aware of it, but if we begin opening ourselves up to the idea then we will see the truth.

As Saint Charan Singh clearly states:

There are no coincidences . . . We call it just coincidence, but there are no coincidences.

The spiritual truth of life, of existence in this world, is that nothing happens that is not meant to happen. In plain language, there simply are no coincidences in this world.

Consider the following quote from Saint Charan Singh:

> *There is no need to worry about anything. We have to face what we have to face. What has to happen has already happened. We can face it cryingly or weepingly or smilingly but we cannot avoid it.*

Note the phrase, "What has to happen has already happened." In other words, what happens is not coincidental. It was destined to happen from the beginning due to our karma. In fact, as Saint Charan Singh declares:

> *Nothing happens without karma.*

We may think that our relationships are a coincidence, but like everything else, they're not. From the Master comes this quote:

> *All these relationships are, in fact, nothing but a settlement of karmic accounts . . . Our karmas bring us together and when they are settled, each one goes his own way.*

Since we may miss the message, he repeats it often in his writings. Here's an example:

> *All our relationships in this world are, in fact, the adjustment of our old karmic debts. When the debtor pays off his debt, he leaves the shell immediately.*

In a fuller description the Master states:

> *All these worldly relationships are meant only for clearing our karmic accounts. Different persons who have karmic accounts to settle with us come into our life as our relatives, friends, acquaintances and so forth, and when their accounts are settled they drift away from us. It*

is our karmas that bring us together and our karmas that separate us from one another. We remain together only as long as we are destined to do so and no more. Sometimes our destiny makes us do things which are much against our wishes. We become a helpless tool in the hands of fate.

He continues:

Our destiny is all marked out and we have to reap what we have sown, then why worry? Face life cheerfully, doing the best you can under the circumstances and then leaving the rest to the Lord.

For those individuals searching for and seeking a spiritual path, Saint Charan Singh explains:

It is not just by coincidence that we come to the Path or to a Master. We are led in that direction. Though we may think it is coincidence, it is as the effect of those karmas that we are automatically led to the Path. Wherever we may be born, ultimately our karma will bring us to the Path when that time comes.

In a shorter version, he says:

Actually, one who is to come to the Path is being guided right from the beginning.

"Right from the beginning." In other words, what was destined to be becomes reality and manifests at the exact moment it was meant to do so. We may think, "What a coincidence," but in reality it was all predetermined from the very beginning.

If you don't believe any of this, then the offer is made once again—study the King's Numerology™ and notice the perfect timing of your numbers with your life's events. You will be stunned to see the perfection. This is because numbers are actually God Codes, the foundation of a divine numeric language.

As we continue to witness the correlation of our numbers with our life's events and relationships, we will come to know, not simply believe, that life is destined—to the breath; that all the events occurring in our life were established before our birth; that life is neither a random happening or a collection of coincidences. Verily, we will learn that there are absolutely no coincidences in our life or anybody's life, and that things which happen "coincidentally" are just another delusion because nothing is coincidental in this world.

There are no coincidences.
We call it just coincidence,
but there are no coincidences.

~ Saint Charan Singh

DELUSION #13

THE #13 IS EVIL

T riskaidekaphobia (pronounced "tris-kahy-dek-uh-foh-bee-uh") is an irrational fear of the number 13 and it is one of the silliest of delusions, if not the silliest.

Somehow this superstition of the #13 being evil or unlucky has transcended the clearheaded attribute of common sense. This irrational fear has so infected our culture that hotels don't even have a 13th floor. Elevators, for example, go from the 12th floor to the 14th floor, skipping the 13th floor. But common sense shines light on this nonsense because what is labeled the 14th floor is, in actuality, the 13th floor. Simply trying to rename something or negate the obvious is ridiculous, illogical and preposterous. It's like trying to rename the sun and opine that it doesn't exist, as if the sun could be negated by simply renaming it. Foolish.

The King's Numerology™ (TKN) explains that all numbers have two sides—one positive, one negative. Therefore, the #13 has a good side and a bad side, so to speak. What the #13 actually represents is transformation, not evil.

If there were no transformation in life, there could be no progress because that which is old and worn out has to be discarded for that which is new. With every breath, for example, we expel used air and take in fresh, life giving oxygen. Used/dead blood in our circulatory system returns to the lungs and heart to become new/living blood and to keep us alive. This is not an evil process; it is a perfectly natural process of simply staying alive.

Death and rebirth are fundamental aspects of life in this creation. Each of our lives is, truly, a constant work of transformation—from cradle to grave. The #13 is one of the numeric energies associated with what Nature has designed for all living beings.

The following excerpt is taken from Chapter 4 of *The King's Book of Numerology, Volume 1 – Foundations and Fundamentals.* (www. RichardKing.net/books)

[Excerpt]
The crown of the number '13' is, of course, '4'. This symbol of security, order and structure is rooted in the '1' of new beginnings and the '3' of integrated perfection. In other words, something new encompasses the integration of the self—the body, mind and spirit—and creates a new understanding of security, a different consciousness of order, a new structure—perhaps a body, perhaps a building, perhaps a code of ethics to live by. When there is something generated which is 'new,' something has to go, has to die, has to be transformed into the new thing. Such is the significance of the number thirteen—the transformer.
[end excerpt]

The King's Numerology™ sees the #13, not as evil but as a regeneration of life itself. The #1 represents action and newness; the #3 signifies perfection; their combination, the #4, identifies structure and form of some kind.

Frankly, the #13 should be welcomed as the energy of "new life" and the eternal process of transformation and regeneration. By not having a 13th floor in hotels or a 13th deck on cruise ships, humans are denying themselves, not just the virtue of having common sense, but the opportunity of realizing and applauding new life.

The #13 numerically represents new life, transformation, and regeneration, not evil.

~ The King's Numerology™

DELUSION #14

OPPOSITES ATTRACT

" **O**pposites attract." How often have we heard this statement? The truth, as far as relationships are concerned, is that opposites may attract temporarily but they don't stay together, nor do they generate harmony but inharmony instead.

What attracts are harmonizing, resonating energies—like-kind, not opposite. Any attraction of opposites is usually a result of ephemeral curiosity. For example, inquisitiveness may unite fire and water briefly but their natural attributes will not just separate them but ultimately destroy them.

A numerology example. The numbers 4 and 5 are exact opposites. The #4 is traditional; the #5 is non-traditional. The #4 loves its security; the #5 adores its freedom. The #4 is practical; the #5 is adventurous. The #4 attaches; the #5 detaches. The #4 is an earth sign; the #5 is a fire sign. In all ways the #4 energy and the #5 energy cancel each other out.

So what happens when a #4 person and #5 person meet? At first, curiosity may attract each to the other because of their intrinsic differences.

However, when the transitory "glow" fades away, the practical-minded #4 will not be able to endure the ever adventurous and impulsive #5. Plus, the #4 is as conventional as it gets while the #5 is the epitome of a free spirit.

Another numerology example, this between the #7 and #8. The #7 is introverted; the #8 is extroverted. The #7 is internalized; the #8 is externalized. The #7 is solitary; the #8 is social. The #7 is the thinker; the #8 is the engager. The #7 can be likened to water receding from the shore back into its source (the ocean) while the #8 rushes to shore to experience the land. At a party, the #7—involved in watching, thinking and observing—is often off to the side or in the background, while the #8 is socializing, mixing with others, shaking hands, engaging, connecting.

So what do you think happens if this #7/#8 couple were to begin a long term relationship? Would it be easy? Natural? Comfortable? Enjoyable? As far as this #7/#8 duo is concerned, it would be a challenge, especially with the #7 seeking privacy while the #8 craves its socialization.

One set of numbers, however, doesn't give a true and clear picture of the #7/#8 relationship because there may be other numbers between each of the partners that override any potential numeric concerns.

For example, in numerology the Soul number is, as far as the King's Numerology[tm] is concerned, the most important number in a numerology chart because the Soul number (based on the vowels—A-E-I-O-U-Y—in the full birth name) defines a person's primal needs, wants, desires, and motivations. It is the engine that gives meaning to other components in the chart, i.e., to the person's life.

Now, what if a #7 Expression individual (the Expression is the name associated with the full birth name) has an #8 Soul? The #7 Expression describes a person in general as a thinker and introvert but his #8 Soul generates a primal desire and need to be an extrovert and socializer. Quite a dilemma, right? A person with a #7 Expression and a #8 Soul will be somewhat perplexed and confused. He/she will be one way on the outside (Expression) but a totally different person on the inside (Soul). This is not uncommon. Many individuals have this #7/#8 conjunction in their charts. Two other conjunctions are the #4/#5, discussed above, and the #1/#2.

Because of these differences, it is critical to understand the dynamics of numbers, especially when it comes to long term relationships such as marriage and business partnerships, as you might surmise.

Another factor of relationships is that individuals often jump into them during a period of time (timeline) that is transitory, only to discover later, when the transitory timeline passes, that the relationship was not as they thought it to be. In fact, it could be just the opposite. As the saying goes, "Haste makes waste," and many marriages and partnerships have fallen apart because this understanding of transitory timelines was not known, understood, or even cast aside, blowing caution to the wind and ultimately reaping the whirlwind.

To ensure a relationship has potential, that there is enough numeric energy to generate an excellent degree of conformity and harmony between the partners, read *Your Love Numbers* or Volume 6 of *The King's Book of Numerology* series, subtitle *Love Relationships*, aka KBN6. Both of these books fully explain how to understand relationships, how to create great relationships and how to even avoid potentially negative relationships using the King's Numerology™ system. The better of the two books is KBN6 because it contains real life examples of marriages that are excellent and marriages that failed. Both books are available at RichardKing.net/books and Amazon.com.

By studying the numbers of relationships, both positive and negative, we can see for ourselves that the quality and duration of relationships depends on the harmony of numbers, not their inharmony. In simple words, like-kind numbers attract, interact and stay intact while disparate numbers reject and disconnect sans short term attraction.

Opposites may attract temporarily but not permanently.

DELUSION #15

IT'S JUST SEX

66 **I**t's just sex." Really? Are you sure? Are you willing to bet your health, well-being, even life on the assumption that sexual relations between people are "just sex."

"It's just sex." Sounds innocuous, doesn't it? No big deal. Why worry? Well, frankly there is a lot to be concerned about when it comes to sex, more than most people understand or realize, especially teenagers.

"It's just sex" is, in fact, one of the most dangerous delusions because of its potentially negative long term effects, both physically and spiritually.

The following three excerpts are taken directly from Chapter 4, "Karma of Free Love" in the book *KARMA-The Definitive Guide to the Supreme Law of this World* (RichardKing.net/books and Amazon.com). They're shared here in an effort to help people understand that the phrase, „It's Just Sex," is a dangerous delusion to one's life.

[Excerpt – KARMA]

THE ENERGY OF CONNECTION

The first thing to realize is that each of us is an energetic being operating within a human body, or more exactly, a human suit. Think of an astronaut. He wears a space suit to protect him from potential dangers, but he is not the suit. The astronaut is a living being housed in a space suit. Likewise, we humans are living energetic beings housed in a human body, a human suit, but we are not our body. This is key. We are energy.

Sexually, when our energies mix with others during sexual intercourse while in a human body we overlook the fact that it is our *energies* that are primarily intermixing. Our bodies are simply the worldly mechanisms facilitating the connection, just as the words on this page are facilitating a message generated by living energy via the mechanism of fingers typing on a material keyboard.

And here's the critical point: while bodies can be separated relatively easily after sexual intercourse, the mixing energies cannot be separated, if at all. This creates massive problems spiritually because our spirits are energy, and the spiritual path focuses on the purification of that energy while the worldly path focuses on the carnal pleasures of the material body.

Think on this metaphor. Take a gallon can of yellow paint, a gallon can of blue paint and mix them thoroughly in a two gallon can. From this admixture, we get two gallons of green paint, right? Now here's the problem: separate the green paint back into its yellow and blue forms. It can't be done. The mixture is permanent.

Likewise, when we mix our energies with those of another person via sexual intercourse, we are generating a third energy which cannot be easily separated. When this process is continually repeated through multiple sexual encounters and partners, massive amounts of karma generate a web of seemingly inextricable energetic entrapment, bondage and imprisonment.

Such karmic loads greatly interfere with our ability to climb the Spiritual Ladder. In fact, they keep us from doing just that, forcing us to become increasingly shackled to this material dimension even more than before we engaged in yet another sexual encounter. In leading such an existence of so called "free love," we have done nothing but add to the fetters of our material and bodily enslavement. Truthfully, indulging in "free love" is not free at all. It is just the opposite, creating karmic chains binding us to this world.

For example, bodies can detach easily, as mentioned, but what about our minds and spirits? Their energy can't detach because the mind houses memories, images, feelings, conversations and a myriad of experiences with every lover we take or have taken. How can all these mental, emotional and psychological entanglements be undone? How can we be free with all the baggage we accumulate from the amalgam of our "free love" interactions? Can we press a magic button in our head that automatically makes us forget about our sexual involvements with others and everything attached to them? No. See the problem? Every sexual lover we have generates its own web of entrapment from which it is practically impossible to escape. To paraphrase Buddha:

Fifty loves, fifty woes. No loves, no woes.

THE DISEASE FACTOR

Furthermore, what about the potential of contracting some sexually transmitted disease or infection which increases the complexity of the karma. The CDC (Centers for Disease Control and Prevention) states, *There are dozens of STDs* and that *20 million new infections occur every year in the United States* (https://www.cdc.gov/std/). STD, of course, stands for sexually transmitted disease. STI stands for sexually transmitted infection. Twenty million new infections every year in the United States alone? What about the rest of the world?

How does any sexually transmitted disease not have a negative impact on someone, let alone millions of people? How much angst, concern, pain, suffering, turmoil, discomfort, sorrow and remorse, etc., are generated by STDs and STIs which, of course, are generally contracted through some form of sexual interaction?

How is having an STD/STI not enslaving? How can one feel free, light-hearted, cheerful, joyful and positive when beset with such diseases? Answer: no one. There is no freedom when struck with any disease. Rather, there is struggle, the degree of which is determined by the severity of the disease. To be sure, "free love" does have its shackles and chains in more ways than one.

The only sure way to be free of the negative effects of today's "free love," promiscuous, permissive lifestyle is to abstain and not engage in sexual intercourse at all. Notwithstanding the pain, angst, turmoil and disease caused by STDs/STIs in both body and mind, what about the immense karmic burden generated in the process? To this point, Guru Nanak remarks: (*Guru Nanak*, p.284)

> *If thou treadest the path of virtue,*
> *sorrow will not dog thy footsteps.*

Guru Ravidas makes a germane point regarding our struggle in these matters of sexuality: (*Guru Ravidas*, p.78)

> *Powerful are our senses and weak is our discrimination,*
> *and spirituality entereth not our understanding.*

In the same work Ravidas states: (Ibid., p.176)

The affliction of lust is the foremost trap of the world. None so entrapped has ever attained the Truth. Why shouldst thou be delighted and comforted in it?

Saint Charan Singh notes: (*Quest for Light*, Letter #492)

Sex is a natural instinct and a powerful one, too. Therefore, the Saints prefer a householder's life where the chances of one going astray from the path of morality are minimized. To stray away from the path of morality results in a very heavy burden, so a controlled householder's life is always preferable. (Note: by "householder's life" is meant a married life).

As a preventive strategy of avoiding the negative aspects of any behavior, Saint Dadu simply says: (*Dadu*, p.18)

Hold pure, stay pure and say pure.
Take the pure, give the pure.

Dadu's advice is simple, direct, effective and truthful. If we always do that which is pure, we will avoid the deleterious effects of impure choices and the heavy karmic burdens associated with them, both in the present and future.

THE DILUTION/POLLUTION FACTOR

Another issue. Even if a person does not contract one of the many debilitating STDs or STIs, there is another potential negative effect confronting those who choose a polyamorous lifestyle—the dilution and pollution of one's own innate energy.

Too, if there were no physical, emotional, psychological, financial or familial problems associated with many loves and lovers, there still remains the karma generated between all parties, karma which will have to be neutralized before we can return Home. Reconciling such Karmic Bonds could take innumerable lives. The fact remains that the more lovers we take, the more vast and intricate our Karmic Web becomes. There's no escaping this reality.

Another important concern involving the Karma of Free Love is that of our purity, wholeness, health and well-being as an individual. When our personal energies mix with those of another individual, they (our energies) become not only diluted but also polluted with the lover's energies, not to mention any physical diseases or infections plaguing the other party which we may contract in the sex act. This Dilution/Pollution Factor generates a double dose of negative karma.

Such a quid-pro-quo of sex and its temporal pleasure in exchange for what we may lose in ourselves, and/or acquire in terms of disease and other problems, is a dangerous and foolish bargain. Is the experience of sexual carnal sensation in a brief encounter really worth the potential cost? Should not the long term risk outweigh the short-lived pleasure? Where is the wisdom of such a choice?

By diluting and adulterating our own energy, we destroy the purity of who we were at birth. With such a continual process of sexual Dilution/ Pollution, we ultimately lose sight and feeling of our intrinsic self and its worth. Eventually, we may not even know ourselves because we have diluted the inherent, pure, natural energy with which we were born.

Where, for example, are the joy-filled, happy, positive, smiling faces in today's society? People are in such a rush, impatient, short-tempered, hostile, angry, even hateful. Is this not, in part, a symptom of today's promiscuous society and the Dilution/Pollution Factor?

Too, this is definitely an age where trust among people in relationships is waning rapidly, is it not? It seems that sleeping with whomever one wishes, whether one is in a relationship or not, overpowers choices of honesty, fidelity, devotion, discipline, self-control, temperance. The lust of passion is dominating a landscape where virtue is almost non-existent. Yet, personal character is of the utmost importance when considering the spiritual life.

Saint Sawan Singh states: (Spiritual Gems, Letter #117)

Purity of character is the fundamental basis on which the edifice of spiritual progress is to be built.

And: (Ibid., Letter #176)

Character is the foundation upon which rises the spiritual edifice. As long as one is a slave of the senses, talk of spirituality is a mockery . . . The first essential step to a spiritual life is character. One may deceive one's friends, relatives, and even oneself but the Power within is not deceived.

Saint Jagat Singh remarks: (The Science of the Soul, p.20)

High moral character is most essential for spiritual progress.

Saint Charan Singh comments: (Divine Light, p.181)

Sex is a natural instinct and to some extent its satisfaction is necessary. But its only purpose, as intended by God, is the procreation and propagation of the species. It should not be made a means of dissolute indulgence and pleasure, as that causes great degradation of the mind, soul and character. A disciplined life is always best.

And: (Ibid., p.300)

> *A high moral character is a condition precedent to God-Realization. Lust and love of God are poles apart and cannot remain together in a man's heart. When one comes, the other goes.*

And: (*Quest for Light*, Letter #221)

> *The first prerequisite of a gentleman or a lady is a good moral character. If that is not there, what else is left?*

The great Helen Keller remarks:

> *Character cannot be developed in ease and quiet. Only through experience of trial and suffering can the soul be strengthened, ambition inspired, and success achieved.*

Famous American political figure and First Lady of the United States, Eleanor Roosevelt, affirms:

> *Only a man's character is the real criterion of worth.*

Where in today's world is character placed on the pedestal requisite to its value? It may be a fair question to ask if the majority of people even place character on a pedestal or in a high position relative to their needs. We may talk about character, but do we honestly practice it and place it in its rightful position of life's priorities, i.e., at the top? Talk is cheap; walking our talk is difficult but obligatory if our goal is Divine Ascent.

Truly, character is critical to our well-being and an antidote to the Dilution/Pollution dilemma. And what is the foundation of character? Answer: virtue in all its forms including discipline, trust, devotion and fidelity.

[end excerpt-KARMA]

After reading this excerpt, can we honestly say regarding sexual intercourse that, "It's just sex." The answer, "No." It's really not. It's much more than just sex, and those who are wise will heed this message and awaken to the reality that the saying, "It's just sex" is a dangerous delusion.

DELUSION #16

IT'S YOUR FAULT

I blame not another. I blame my own karmas.
Whatever I sowed, so did I reap.
Why then put the blame on others?
~ Guru Nanak

A rguably, the greatest hindrance to personal responsibility, accountability and maturity is the delusion, "It's your fault." Blaming others for our missteps, mistakes, faults, failings, sins and shortcomings is rampant in today's world.

It is so very tiring to see individuals constantly blaming others for their (the doer's) own actions. It is a fair question to ask, "When will the mass of humanity start growing up and place the blame on themselves for their own bad actions rather than trying to shuffle them off to someone else?"

Furthermore, it is especially tiring to see adults, or rather people masquerading as adults, engage in such immature and childish behavior. At such adolescent conduct, one can only scream, "Grow Up!"

"Grown ups, own up." It doesn't matter the age. A ten year old child who has been taught to take responsibility for himself and his actions is far more "adult" than a 30s, 40s, 50s, 60s, 70s, 80s, etc., individual who has never learned to be accountable for his/her actions.

Ask yourself, "How many times have you seen or heard someone say, 'It's my fault,' or the vernacular, 'My bad?'" It is more likely to see individuals own up to their own mistakes in the world of sport but where else? Politics? Never. CEOs? Seldom, if ever. We could go on but you get the picture. Publically standing up and owning up to one's mistakes are rare.

The thing is, we all make mistakes, so why not just espouse the obvious, i.e., "Sorry. I messed up," rather than trying to blame someone else for our bloopers, blunders, gaffes, faux pas, snafus and a whole host of other flub-ups? Most of us would be quite forgiving if someone owned up to their negative actions because we all know we all make them. Nobody's perfect. Yet, it is stunning how so many people refuse to do so. They just can't admit to the truth of their actions. This is sad and unfortunate.

But here's the reality: We sow, we reap, and we cannot reap what we do not sow. All Saints and Mystics understand this, so why not the common man?

As Guru Nanak states:

> I blame not another. I blame my own karmas. Whatever I sowed, so did I reap. Why then put the blame on others?

The most evolved souls, being the most enlightened and adult, never blame anyone else for their misdeeds, were they to make them. They only blame themselves, like Guru Nanak stated.

The following excerpt is from pages 75 and 76 of *Parenting Wisdom: What to Teach the Children*, available at RichardKing.net/books & Amazon.com.

[Excerpt]

So it goes with all highly evolved souls. They understand that what happens to them is by their own hand, by their own doing. They never blame others because to blame others would be to deny the science and reality of life. Saints know, and all mature individuals know, that to be an adult means to take responsibility for oneself and one's actions, i.e., Grown Ups, Own Up.

It may seem obvious that adult individuals own up to their own lives and actions, but is this true? How many Grown Ups actually own up to their lives, choices, circumstances, responsibilities, obligations, financial conditions, and relationship interactions? Furthermore, and more importantly, how many Grown Ups are truly accountable and responsible for their mistakes, faults, failings, and shortcomings?

We live in an age where owning up seems to be a dying virtue, like so many other virtues. It's so easy to pass the buck and blame someone else. We see such adolescent behavior in all walks of life and even at the pinnacle of those in the hallowed halls of leadership. And that is exactly what passing the buck is—adolescent. It is not adult behavior. It is childish behavior. Just because a person lives in a biologically adult body does not make him or her an adult. Why? Because Grown Ups, Own Up, and being "grown up" means owning up and being accountable for one's actions.

[end excerpt]

It is a major delusion to think that our negative behavior is someone else's fault. Whom do we think we're fooling? Answer: only ourselves. By blaming someone else rather than ourselves, we're showing the entire world how childish, adolescent and immature we are. Nobody can fault us for telling the truth but we surely make fools of ourselves when we attempt to pass the buck off to someone else for our actions. The quicker we can dissolve this delusion within us, the quicker we'll move toward being an upright, honest and substantive individual.

I blame not another.
I blame my own karmas.
Whatever I sowed, so did I reap.
Why then put the blame on others?

~ Guru Nanak

DELUSION #17

IT DOESN'T MATTER WHAT YOU EAT

Actually, what we eat does matter a great deal, especially if we're following or would like to follow the Spiritual Path. All diets do not have the same effect on the human body, nor do they bear the same consequences of the human spirit.

For example, someone adopting an omnivorous diet (all kinds of foods—animal and plant life) has no limits on his choices. However, a vegetarian diet is absolutely requisite if one desires to pursue the Spiritual Journey. As Saint Jagat Singh states:

> As long as one does not give up the animal diet, one cannot begin the spiritual journey.

Why is this? It is because eating the flesh of animals, birds, fish and insects involves killing, which subsequently generates massive karmic debt and its reconciliation.

As Saint Charan Singh admonishes:

If we kill we must be killed. We must never forget that.

This is a direct reference to the Law of Karma which returns to us the exact act of our own doing.

As the Bible states in Galatians 6:7:

Be not deceived; God is not mocked, for whatsoever a man soweth, that shall he also reap.

Underscore *that*, which in this case means the "same." Therefore, if we kill we must be killed according to Karmic Law, whether it is in this life or the next life or the life after that. Eventually, the debt of killing will come due and we will have to pay *that* debt with our own life, and it won't be fun. The more killing we do, the more killing we will have to endure. Like it or not; believe it or not, this is the truth of this creation. If we kill, how then can we advance up the Divine Ladder? As long as we're chained to this world with the "fetters of flesh," we'll never be able to escape it, which is in direct contrast to the purpose of the Spiritual Journey, which is to take us Home and away from this very dark world.

And then there is the aspect of love, not just for man, but for all living things. Speaking of the vegetarian diet, Saint Charan Singh remarks:

We must follow it. There is no other way for spiritual progress . . . If we kill, we will be killed. We should never forget that. Christ said, "Love thy neighbor." All creatures are our neighbors . . . When you love anybody, you do not kill that individual; and when we love the whole creation, we cannot kill intentionally nor could we find it in our heart to have it done for us by someone else.

The following quote is from *Liberation of the Soul* by Saint Charan Singh. It will startle many people. Its genesis is from *The Essene Gospel of St. John, Dead Sea Scrolls, Chapter XXII* in which Christ is speaking.

> *Kill not, neither eat the flesh of your innocent prey lest you become the slaves of Satan. For that is the path of suffering and it leads unto death. Obey, therefore, the words of God: 'Behold, I have given you every herb bearing seed which is upon the face of all the earth and every tree in which is the fruit of a tree yielding seed; to you it shall be for meat.' [Christ is referring to the Biblical commandment from Genesis, Chapter 1].*

Christ continues:

> *And to every beast of the earth and to every fowl of the air and to everything that creepeth upon the Earth wherein is breath of life, I give every green herb for meat.*

> *Also the milk of everything that moveth and liveth upon earth shall be meat for you.*

> *But flesh and blood which quickens it, shall ye not eat. And surely, your spurting blood will I require, your blood wherein is your soul. I will require all slain beasts, and the souls of all slain men.*

> *For I, the Lord thy God, am a God strong and jealous, visiting the iniquity of the fathers upon the children unto the third and fourth generation of them that hate me and showing mercy unto thousands of them that love me and keep my commandments.*

> *Do you not understand that those others are you yourself? You yourself will reap what you sow, not others!*

He who kills a beast without cause, though the beast attack him not, through lust for slaughter or for its flesh or its hide or yet for its tusks, evil is the deed which he does for he is turned into a wild beast himself. Wherefore is his end also as the end of the wild beast.

God commanded your forefathers: Thou shall not kill. But their hearts were hardened and they killed. Then Moses desired that at least they should not kill men and he suffered them to kill beasts. And the heart of your forefathers was hardened, yet more, they killed men and beasts likewise. But I say unto you: Kill neither men, nor beasts, nor yet the food which goes into your mouth. For if you eat living food, the same will quicken you, but if you kill your food, the dead food will kill you also. For life comes only from life, and from death comes always death. For everything which kills your food, kills your body also. And everything which kills your bodies, kills your souls also.

From the book *Jesus, The Gospel of Peace*, we read:

And the flesh of slain beasts in his body will become his tomb. For I tell you truly, he who kills, kills himself, and whoso eats the flesh of slain beasts, eats the body of death.

The book *Jesus, The Gospel of the Holy Twelve*, makes this statement:

God giveth the grains and the fruits of the earth for food, and for a righteous man truly there is no other lawful sustenance for the body.

Bible, Romans 14:21 contains this passage:

It is better not to eat meat or drink wine or to do anything else that will cause any man to stumble.

Of course there will be individuals who believe Christ ate fish, which runs counter to him being a vegetarian. However, according to TheNazareneWay.com, there are scholars who contend that the word "fish" mentioned in the 14th Chapter of St. Matthew (verses 13-21) was actually a reference to "fish weed" (dried seaweed), which was a popular food among Palestinian peasants. This makes much more sense in keeping with Christ's message of love for all living things.

It's very clear from these passages that Christ was a vegetarian, and his life of love for all living beings, whether animal or human, was the same. For one to preach love and slay living beings, would make such a person a hypocrite. Christ was no hypocrite but true to his ethos of love for all souls.

Following are a few more vegetarian quotes from Saints.

Saint Dariya of Bihar shares these direct thoughts:

> By consuming meat, fish and wine, one is defiled and incurs enormous sins . . . One incurs an enormous sin by killing a single living being . . . Just as our own life is dear to us, so is life dear to all other beings . . . He who inflicts blows and kills living beings will have to suffer tortures in the end . . . Knowing your own child to be happy, you embrace him with delight, but you peel off the skin of others for which you will suffer the same fate . . . Shedding of others' blood is paid for with one's own blood. Such is the law . . . Those who eat meat and fish are persons of the lowest class . . . By consuming meat, fish and wine, one is defiled and incurs enormous sins.

Here are a few quotes from Saint Sawan Singh:

> I must point out that animal food, even if a single particle is eaten, is detrimental to spiritual progress . . . To kill an animal is a heinous

*offense under natural law and its punishment is very severe. The
Saints have strictly forbidden taking any sort of life in any way.*

Tukaram, the Saint of Maharashtra, remarks:

*Men who presume that creatures have no life and cut their throats,
are selfish and heartless and incur great sin. The Lord dwells within
every being. Does man not know that He resides in animals, too? In
his very presence the creatures scream in agony; still man raises his
hand to kill them. Says Tuka, such a vile one will have to suffer. He
will be hurled into the fires of hell.*

From Saint Namdev come these thoughts:

*Like his own child, man nurses the young one of a beast but thrusts
a knife to kill it, to serve as meat. When the noose is round his
own neck, he cries in anguish; but he hesitated not when he inflicted
mortal blows. Says Nama, shameless creatures that they are, how
can they ever hope to realize the Lord?*

Saint Dadu comments:

*If anyone takes the life of any other creature, that person goes to
hell. I tell you the truth. There is no doubt about it, sayeth Dadu . .
. Whatever beings thou killest, the same ones will kill thee in turn.
Whatever beings thou savest, the same ones will save thee in return.*

Tulsi Sahib, Saint of Hathras observes:

*They verily fall into the dungeon of hell who slaughter living beings
and eat their flesh . . . For the sake of sensual gratification they buy
sin and get their abode in the fires of hell . . . Tulsi declares from the*

housetops: kill not the living; within all resides the beloved Lord—
listen, O men and women!

Saint Kabir notes:

And I entreat you, take this fact to heart: that he whom you so
lightly kill today, will someday slaughter you.

Saint Ravidas says:

Kill not thou any living beings. Living beings veritably are one with
God . . . He who ever eats cows and goats for the sake of nourishing
his body, he can never go to heaven, O Ravidas, even if he offers holy
prayers day and night.

The great thing about Saints is that they're very direct and tell the truth, even if the truth is difficult to accept. We have to remember that the Saints' message is to purify the soul, not make people feel good about their material and carnal habits.

It doesn't take a Saint to understand the vegetarian lifestyle. Following are some quotes from normal human beings.

George Bernard Shaw:

Animals are my friends; I don't eat my friends . . . We are the graves
of murdered beasts slaughtered to satisfy our appetites.

Mohandas Gandhi:

I do not regard flesh-food as necessary for us at any stage and under
any clime in which it is possible for human beings ordinarily to live.
I hold flesh-food to be unsuited to our species. We err in copying the
lower animal world—if we are superior to it.

To my mind, the life of a lamb is no less precious than that of a human being. I should be unwilling to take the life of a lamb for the sake of the human body.

Paul McCartney:

If slaughterhouses had glass walls, everyone would be vegetarian.

Dr. Albert Schweitzer, Nobel Peace Laureate:

To me, ethics is nothing else than reverence for life. Reverence for life affords me my fundamental principal of morality, namely, that good consists in maintaining, assisting and enhancing life, and that to destroy, to harm or to hinder life is evil.

Buddha:

To become vegetarian is to step into the stream which leads to nirvana.

Pythagoras:

As long as man continues to be the ruthless destroyer of lower living beings, he will never know health or peace.

That pretty well puts to bed the delusion that *It Doesn't Matter What You Eat.* What we eat does matter, massively. All diets do not lead in the same direction, to the same place. As human beings, we would be wise and well-served to adopt a vegetarian diet, especially if we want to rise into Divine Realms and live in the Light that is Love.

DELUSION #18

THERE IS ONLY ONE SAVIOR

How can there be only one Son of God? One Savior for all mankind? Christians have Christ; Muslims have Muhammad. However, is God so limited, so capricious, so unkind that He would restrict Himself to only having one son? One savior? Such a concept limits God, making him limited, not limitless.

To think that in the entire universe there is only one Savior for all people for all time is not only delusional but preposterous, and lacks basic common sense.

At the time of this writing in the year 2021, there are close to eight billion people living on the face of the earth (www.worldometers.info/world-population), none of whom were alive during the lives of Jesus or Muhammad. How is it therefore possible to have direct interactions with these religious Icons and receive the benefit of their presence and spirituality?

There are those individuals who believe, for example, that Jesus was the only Son of God . . . for all time. Common sense challenges this statement. Do we really believe that God, who created Jesus and Muhammad, would condemn billions of souls because they have different beliefs or religious opinions?

Here's a critical note regarding the phrase from St. John 3:16:

> *For God so loved the world, that he gave his only begotten Son, that whosoever believeth in him should not perish, but have everlasting life.*

The language of Jesus was Aramaic. In an interview on television circa 1978 (apologies for not remembering the show), an Aramaic scholar said that the above phrase contained a transposition of the words "his only" which should be "only his." The actual phrase from John 3:16 should then read:

> *For God so loved the world, that he gave only his begotten Son, that whosoever believeth in him should not perish, but have everlasting life.*

This error has confused many souls but when the transposition is corrected, the quote from John 3:16 makes total sense.

In the Bible, St. John 9:5, Christ himself said:

> *As long as I am in the world, I am the light of the world.*

Jesus never said he was the light of the world forever.

And then we have to consider the size of our own Milky Way. Astronomers guess there are anywhere from 100 billion stars to 700 billion stars in the galaxy. There have to be living beings on various worlds in those star systems, intelligent beings like us, so are all those beings doomed because they are not from earth and didn't live in the time of Christ or Muhammad?

Continuing along this line of thought, there are believed to be around two trillion galaxies in the known universe (www.worldatlas.com). How many worlds supporting life are contained in these 2,000,000,000,000 galaxies?

Furthermore, NASA estimates the known universe is 13.8 billion years old (www.space.com). What is the potential of living beings inhabiting the incredible number of worlds in the universe and for all time? Answer: huge!

Common sense tells us that as great as Jesus, Muhammad, Kabir, Nanak, Dadu, Dariya and other spiritual Icons were, there would have to be other Sons of God existing on other worlds at other times in the history of the universe. It is simply not plausible to believe that Almighty God would only create one or two of his sons to serve as spiritual servants of the masses. It fact, it is delusional.

From the book, *With The Three Masters*, (Volume 2, 4th Edition, 2001, published by Sewa Singh, Secretary, Radha Soami Satsang Beas; page 10), we read:

> *How deluded are those men who, pinning their faith on their traditional religions, are depending upon the founders of those religions who died thousands of years ago, to come and give them salvation.*

Obviously, clear thinking says they cannot. The connection between Master and disciple must be made when both are living and occupying a human body.

Saints say there is always at least one Son of God on the planet at any one time, which makes perfect spiritual sense.

From *Kabir, The Great Mystic,* we read:

> *There can be no single savior for the whole world for all times and till the end of time.*

From *Guru Nanak, His Mystic Teachings,* we learn this:

> *Of their being only one master in the history of the world: God, who is just and all merciful, would not dispense His mercy in so capricious a manner. He would not confine His saints to a brief period and debar those born earlier or later from attaining salvation and union with Him . . . The Lord, in fact, has been all-merciful in His grace. He has so ordained that the world will never be without saints. This is a divine law, which, unlike social or political laws, cannot be changed. Those who seek union with Him will always have a master to help and guide them.*

Guru Nanak continues:

> *Past masters. . . cannot take us to the transcendent regions now, nor can they give us any guidance in our spiritual journey within. Says Saint Sawan Singh:*

All Saints are Sons of God . . . Saints are always present in the world.

Swami Ji Maharaj remarks:

> *In short, it is impossible for anyone to attain salvation by simply believing in or worshipping a Saint, prophet, incarnation or god who lived in the past.*

And as a final remark, Saint Charan Singh clearly states:

The world is never without saints.

Another delusion dissolved.

DELUSION #19

ONLY JESUS ASCENDED

One of the most miraculous and provocative events in world history, especially in the Christian community, is that of Christ's resurrection from the tomb after his crucifixion.

There is a belief that Jesus has been the only person to have such an experience, but such is not the case. Guru Nanak and Saint Kabir also manifested similar experiences upon their "passing." The event of Christ's resurrection is, arguably, more well known because of the way he was tortured and crucified.

This revelation of the miraculous "passing" of Guru Nanak and Saint Kabir is certainly not meant to diminish or disparage Christ's resurrection. It is simply offered to expand the reality of the universality of spiritual and mystical events.

Born on 15 April 1469, Guru Nanak was the founder of Sikhism and is the first and best known of the Ten Sikh Gurus whose holy text is the Guru Granth Sahib.

Nanak, whose life is celebrated globally by his Sikh, Hindu and Muslim followers, was a supreme mystic. During his life he traveled extensively across Asia, spreading the message of one God who dwells within us all.

As Nanak was preparing to leave his body before the day of his passing (22 September 1539 at age 70), his followers argued as to who would claim his body for funeral rites. The Sikh and Hindu custom is to cremate the body, while the Muslim tradition is to bury the corpse.

As the story goes, in order to settle the dispute of his followers, Nanak directed them to each bring flowers to lay in his bed. Sikhs and Hindus were to place their flowers on his right side; Muslims were to place theirs on his left side. After a prayer session, Nanak had his followers place a sheet over his entire body, asking them to depart until the next morning, telling them that whosever's flowers were the freshest when everyone gathered the next morning, they could claim his body and dispose of it per their customs. When his Sikh, Hindu and Muslim followers returned the next morning and removed the sheet from his body, there was no body! Only flowers, fresher than before, remained in the bed. In effect, Guru Nanak had "evaporated," in a similar manner as had Christ.

Saint Kabir's passing was very much akin to that of Nanak's. In his book *Kabir, The Weaver of God's Name*, author V.K. Sethi gives us a glimpse of Kabir in the first paragraph of his Preface:

> *Kabir, the fifteenth-century Saint of Banaras, was a low-caste weaver with no formal education; his humble origin did not prevent him, however, from becoming renowned in his own lifetime as a great Saint, and his compositions were recited, as they are now, all over the country. Of all the mystics of India, Kabir is perhaps the most well known worldwide.*

When Kabir was in the process of leaving this world, his Hindu and Muslim followers, like those of Guru Nanak, fought over who should claim Kabir's body after he was gone. Hindus wanted to cremate it; Muslims to bury it per their separate traditions.

As Kabir's story unfolds, and when the time for him to "die" was at hand, Kabir retired to his hut, giving instructions to his followers that he was not to be disturbed. When inside, he covered himself with a white cloth from head to toe. After a time, his followers became concerned and entered his hut only to find a white sheet but no body! Kabir, like Jesus and Nanak, had made a grand and miraculous exit from this world.

What these accounts of Jesus, Nanak and Kabir tell us is that there is much we normal humans do not understand about life and the powers that dwell within us. If these three transcendent Souls can manifest such power, then so can we. Christ himself confirms this in John 14:12:

> *Verily, verily, I say unto you, He that believeth on me, the works that I do shall he do also; and greater works than these shall he do; because I go unto my Father.*

Underscore two phrases:

> *The works that I do shall he do also.*

and...

> *Greater works than these shall he do.*

There's much to ponder here, especially the concept of "Greater works."

DRUGS CREATE SPIRITUAL EXPERIENCES

This delusion can be put to bed right away. Drugs, especially recreational drugs including marijuana, which are the focus of this section, may create psychological experiences of various types and degrees but such experiences are not spiritual. As Saint Charan Singh emphatically states in "Quest For Light:"

Love of God is not obtained by drugs.

Spiritual experiences transcend material experiences. When an individual is high on drugs, having hallucinations, seeing colors, visions, etc., he may think he's having spiritual experiences but he's not. It's only a delusion.

Even if an individual is under the influence of alcohol—a drug—he may not be having hallucinations but he may be physically, psychologically and emotionally impaired to the point of injuring himself and/or others. As far as the Spiritual Path is concerned, the full scope of recreational drugs including alcohol, hemp and marijuana are a major no-no. As Saint Kabir clearly states:

If you wish to meet the Lord, you must give up all liquor, opium, bhang, tobacco. That is a pre-condition.

Saint Dariya of Bihar exclaims:

How can there be wisdom when one takes delight in hemp and marijuana?

This is interesting because Dariya lived in the 17th/18th Centuries and the fact that he mentions marijuana back then shows how powerful and destructive it was even in his time.

Dariya also includes wine in his caveats.

Only if you wish to be drowned in the dreadful ocean of the world, may you drink wine. The ocean ahead is indeed fearsome. You will weep and wail later on.

Obviously, Saint Dariya, as well as other Saints, is serious about following the Spiritual Path. He and they pull no punches. They simply tell it like it is—like it or not.

Sadly, recreational drug usage worldwide is increasing, not decreasing. Statista.com shares these facts:

From 1999 to 2019, the number of drug overdose deaths among U.S. females increased from 5,591 in 1999 to 22,426 in 2019. Globally, drug use is a general problem. In 2017, it was estimated that over half of all adults globally had used illegal drugs in their lifetime. As of 2018, there were an estimated 269 million global drug consumers and 35.6 million drug addicts.

OurWorldInData.org offers the following data:

Collectively, smoking, alcohol and illicit drug use kills 11.8 million people each year. This is more than the number of deaths from all cancers.

The Centers for Disease Control and Prevention (cdc.gov) states:

Over 81,000 drug overdose deaths occurred in the United States in the 12 months ending in May 2020, the highest number of overdose deaths ever recorded in a 12-month period according to recent provisional data from the Centers for Disease Control and Prevention.

Nymag.com gives us this startling fact:

2020 . . . is on track to be the deadliest year for U.S. drug overdose deaths in recorded history.

Underscore "in recorded history."

This does not speak well to the consciousness level of us earthlings. Rather, it reveals how magnetized we are to the material world and its carnal seduction.

To repeat Guru Nanak's warnings:

Precious is the human birth; only the saints know its worth.

And . . .

> *Men are victims of their evil passions and are dominated by their worldly attachments. They forget that the human birth is a very rare gift, the only one in eighty-four lakhs of species for attaining release from birth and death.*

Recalling the Biblical admonition: (1 Corinthians 3:16)

> *Know ye not that ye are the temple of God and that the Spirit of God dwelleth in you? If any man defile the temple of God, him shall God destroy, for the temple of God is holy, which temple ye are.*

Do you remember this quote from Saint Charan Singh?

> *The human body is not given to us in every birth. We get it only after millions of lives, and it is a very rare and precious gift not to be wasted upon the perishable things and objects of this world.*

How very tragic it is for so many millions of individuals to throw away their very precious and rare human life for the sake of ephemeral and destructive material/carnal pleasure! It is, to be sure, a tragedy beyond words.

To be extremely clear, recreational drugs, alcohol, hemp, marijuana, etc. are demonic. They not only destroy the body and its potential but the soul as well. To think for a nano second that drugs create spiritual experiences is a deadly delusion in more ways than one. If we're wise, we'll take this knowledge to heart and steer clear of these evil substances. They certainly do not serve our highest and best good, let alone the potential of spiritual ascendance.

DELUSION #21

GHOSTS AREN'T REAL

G hosts exist. They're referred to as "discarnate entities," i.e., spirits (people) without a physical body. There are those who state that ghosts aren't real; that they're just a figment of the imagination; that people who believe in ghosts are crazy or simply misinformed. Understandable, but simply not true. Frankly, those people who don't believe in ghosts have never encountered one. If they had, they wouldn't be denouncing their existence. This author, in fact, has been in two "haunted houses" and he can testify by experience that ghosts are real.

Regarding ghosts, Saint Sawan Singh says:

Just as there are angels, there are ghosts. They are residents of the astral plane . . . People who are very much given over to sexual and other low desires and have not been able to satisfy their cravings usually incarnate as ghosts. As disembodied forms, they attach themselves to weak folk having low desires. They do not go near strong-minded persons.

And . . .

Souls that are in the astral region sometimes manifest themselves to souls on the physical plane, but they cannot harm the souls on the physical plane in any way. Only superstitious and weak-minded persons are liable to be frightened by these apparitions.

And . . .

Ghosts and evil spirits harass only those weak-minded persons who are afraid of them. They cannot do any harm to a person who is not afraid of them.

In the book *With The Three Masters* (Volume 2, 4th Edition, 2001, published by Sewa Singh, Secretary, Radha Soami Satsang Beas; pages 12 to 14), it is said:

That one who dies thinking strongly of a house becomes a ghost in the next birth.

The passage continues, describing an account of a wise and learned man who actually conversed with a ghost in a room of a certain residence. The ghost had been a holy man in his past life. The man was able to help the ghost escape from his ghostly body. It's a fascinating read. Following is the ghost's account of how he became a ghost.

I live in an alcove of this room. I was the last Mahant (holy man in charge) of the Dharamshala (district headquarters of Kangra district of Himachal Pradesh, India) and my end came when I was building a room in the upper storey of this house. My last thoughts were about this uncompleted room, and therefore I became a ghost in this building.

Saint Sawan Singh, in hearing of this story, said:

Many souls like that of this good and wise Mahant are wandering around in every part of this world. There may be many in this very room.

Sawan Singh stated that there was also a ghost living in a tree on the other side of his residence for fourteen/fifteen years and that the ghost was actually guarding the residence so no harm would befall it. He did say that generally ghosts only go to drunkards, sinners and other wicked men and women.

[Personal note]

Since I stated I have been in two "haunted" houses, it's only fair I share some details of these experiences.

In the first instance, I was house-sitting for a friend in 1981. The day I arrived, as I was standing in the entrance hall of the home, there was a huge bang in the kitchen. The entrance hall and kitchen were separated by a wall. The "bang" sounded like a football fullback blasting through the defensive line of his opponent. I went into the kitchen thinking something fell off a table. Nothing did. Then, as I was standing by the door leading to the garage, the "bang" happened again. I opened the door immediately but, alas!, there was nothing there! How could that be? I had opened that door within two seconds of hearing the bang. I ran out the side door to the garage but saw no one. I then ran back through the house and out the front door but saw nothing again. Things were getting very mysterious, not to mention strange.

Later that day, a friend came by to visit for a few minutes and after she left she called me and asked who was in the front bedroom because just before she drove away she saw the window curtain, which had been pulled aside, fall back down. I told her no one was in that bedroom. I now started to get suspicious—first the kitchen door bangs, twice, and I could find no answer as to what caused it, and now this—a curtain falling in a bedroom where no one was present.

That night, Saturday, as I slept, I was startled and awakened by someone shoving the left side of the bed on which I was sleeping at 1:12 AM. I instantly popped up, ready to do battle, but no one was there! As I lay back down, I heard sounds like furniture moving in the attic. At that point, I became concerned and slept with the lights on. Things were getting really creepy and spooky.

The next night, Sunday, as I was sleeping, I felt someone sit down on the end of the bed. It was 1:15 AM, a similar time to the previous night's episode. I popped up and, again, no one was there! Creepy, creepy. I laid back down and, once again, the same noises started coming from the attic and I most definitely wasn't going to go up and find out what they were.

The next day I received a call from my friend, checking up on me and asking how I was doing. I responded by telling him that I thought he had a ghost in his house. He responded immediately by saying, and I'll never forget his exact words, "Thank God somebody else finally knows!" He then went on to describe things that he and his three children had personally witnessed regarding the ghost.

Since my friend corroborated my experiences with his own, I decided to do some research on that house. It turns out that a husband committed suicide in the attic by hanging himself after discovering his wife was having an affair. That explained everything.

This house-sitting adventure was the first ghostly event in my life, but it wasn't going to be the last.

My second haunted house adventure was more personal. It happened in a home I shared with my second wife and our four girls (two from each of our prior marriages).

It was the holiday season, circa 1991. Our family took a vacation to visit my mom in Northern California. We arrived on a Thursday but the very next day we received word that my wife's mother had suddenly died. We packed up and immediately left to be with her family.

Long story short, all kinds of weird things began to happen in our home. Water faucets would automatically turn on by themselves, books and papers placed neatly in the childcare room were strewn all about the room; the familiar "door banging" (from the last haunted house) also occurred at a time when my wife, our four girls and two other people were standing by the front door where it happened; fragrant aromas were wafting around the bottom of the stairs; the kids would feel cold air brushing by them for no seeable reason; bathroom door handles would rattle up and down when the girls were taking showers and steps could be heard on the balcony outside the master bedroom as well as running across the master bedroom floor. All kinds of weird, unnatural things were happening. Creepy, creepy and more creepy.

The girls were all getting frightened with everything that was happening, so much so that we decided to do some metaphysical work in hopes of solving this ongoing mystery, which had been happening for several months. In the process, we discovered that the ghost in our home was actually my wife's mother! She had been trying to make contact with us after she died so quickly and without saying good-bye.

From that point on ghostly things stopped happening, sort of. For example, Mama Ghost would often be heard walking on the balcony outside our master bedroom. I would say, "Mom, you're scaring everyone so please go back down stairs," and sure enough, she would go back down stairs.

She was probably just checking in to make sure everyone was tucked in properly, as mothers do.

My mother-in-law was a very sweet woman. She was kind, loving, soft-hearted—not a scary ghost at all. Her antics were scary but she was just trying to make contact, which she ultimately did, thanks to her undying persistence.

Then one day my father-in-law came by to visit. When he left, Mama Ghost must have gone with her husband because all of the "spooky experiences" in the house stopped from that point on. Certainly, it was a lovely finale to a ghostly adventure, proving that ghosts are indeed real.

DELUSION #22

IT WILL BE ALL RIGHT

It Will Be All Right is a phrase often used by someone to comfort someone else who has experienced a tragedy, loss, or difficult event. But is it a delusion? It's not a delusion if what happened does turn out to be all right. However, if what happened doesn't turn out to be all right, and there was no way it could ever be, then yes, *It Will Be All Right* can be considered a delusion—a false belief held to be true but isn't.

For example what happens if a wife's husband or a husband's wife is killed and some well-intentioned person tells the bereft individual that "It will be all right" when certainly it won't be? The statement then was delusional from the beginning and could be considered a disservice to the bereaved person or other affected individuals, such as family members and close friends. How does it help someone feel comforted when they're told that "It will be all right" when it is impossible for it to never be right?

This is certainly not to disparage the individual who is trying to help. Such a person's intent is to be warm, reassuring, caring. This said, shouldn't we be more observant and judicious of our words telling someone "it will be all right" when we know there's no way it can be?

Would it not be better to say, "I'm so sorry for your loss. How can I help you?"

Or ...

I know this is heartbreaking for you but I'm here to help and I'll do everything I can to minimize your pain and suffering.

Or ...

I'm here for you. What do you need me to do? What can I do? How can I be of service?

Anyone who has seen a great deal of death knows that things may never be all right from that moment on. Losing a partner, parent, friend, child or family member will generate agony beyond words. Therefore, a person whose life has been forever changed by some tragic event needs love and support, not clichés, platitudes or delusionary statements.

If we're the person who has suffered a great loss, then we need to do our best to remain calm, be balanced and centered, not only for ourselves but for others around us, such as children.

There have been incidents where a parent loses his/her spouse, and totally falls apart, forgetting their obligation to their children who are hurting as much or more than the widowed parent. This is very sad and tragic. And if the parent never "gets it together," perhaps becoming an alcoholic or drug addict in an attempt to neutralize their pain and suffering, the children can be scarred for life. Parents need to understand this. Their obligations are to care for the children first, to give them love, nurturing and support because they're the most innocent and vulnerable. It is hard to do, of course, but parents must be parents and look to their children's needs first in spite of their (the parent's) pain, anguish and suffering.

This scenario of any family member dying is not uncommon. Just turn on the TV. Every day people die, many of whom died tragically and left an entire family behind. For them, it will never be all right, and to say that "It will be all right" is not what needs to be said because if you've lived it, you know your life will never be the same. It will never be all right.

Two of the hardest hit sections of our society which have experienced such tumult, tragedy and eternal pain and suffering are law enforcement and the military. If you've served or been a family member of one who served, perhaps even died, you fully understand what is being said. Your sacrifice often goes unnoticed by the masses who take your protective services for granted. This book understands your sacrifice and salutes you for all that you have done for others, for the services you have rendered.

If there is any hope that "It will be all right," then that hope has to come from within the individual. He or she must acquire a strong backbone, positive attitude and adapt a "never give in" and "never give up" disposition. It's an inevitable battle between external tragedies and internal realities—a personal, silent war. The way to conquer such a condition is to realize the Divinity Within. Go there! Rest there! Be blessed there! Never be shy about asking God for help.

When tragedy strikes us and we are overwhelmed with pain, sorrow, suffering, grief and uncertainty, we need to gather as much strength as we can and remain as balanced and centered as we can. We can't undo the tragedy that befell us, but we can keep things from becoming worse and getting out of control by not "losing it."

Furthermore, if we have children and our spouse dies, we need to remember the children are hurting, too. As parents, we are duty-bound to care for our young before we care for ourselves. We can't change the past, but we can certainly ensure that the future is not saturated with more suffering than that which exists in the "now." It's not easy, granted, but it's deeply important. If a parent falls totally apart and fails to render solace and nurturing to the children, the children could be scarred for life. Therefore, in spite of our own suffering, we must "keep it together" for our kids and not abandon them in their pain and anguish. Things may never be all right again but we need to do our best to make sure they won't be worse.

It would also be helpful to remember that everything in this world has two sides—one positive, one negative. Therefore, as challenging as a tragedy may be, there is an opposite side to its anguish. What is that side? It may not be readily apparent in the present atmosphere of "hurt," but it has to be there by natural law. What is it? Where is the blessing?

Too, it would also be helpful to remember that whatever happened had to happen by karmic law. There are no accidents in this world. None. Can we learn to be at peace with this natural law? Remember, we may wail, scream and blame God for our pain and suffering but our pain and suffering are due to our own actions in previous lives.

None of us is innocent or undeserving of what befalls us. In managing any crisis, it would behoove us to dwell on this most important aspect of living in this creation. As there are no accidents in this world, there are also no innocent victims in this world. If we're to live a balanced life, with all of its pain and suffering, we need to address this fact of personal accountability and responsibility. When that occurs, then everything will be all right because we will live in Truth, not delusion.

DELUSION #23

EVERYONE HAS A SOUL MATE

There exists a thought that everyone in this world has a soul mate, a person who is their perfect match. This is yet another delusion, most likely developed to assuage people's desire to have someone they can call their own. The Saints' point of view is different. They proclaim there is no such thing as a soul mate, that each individual is following an independent course.

Says Saint Charan Singh:

> *The soul has no soul-mate and the soul has no sex . . . The soul does not need nor can it have a soul-mate at all. Every soul is individual. We have our individual relation with the Lord. We do not need to get somebody . . . Absolutely, we have no soul-mate. We are working our way back to the Lord independently.*

Knowing this truth will keep people from hoping or wanting what can never be; will never be. Thus, they can exist from a more wholeness-engendering concept and not waste their lives in delusion.

In speaking of worldly relationships, and as we learned in Delusion #12, "Things Happen Coincidentally," Saint Charan Singh remarks:

All these relationships are, in fact, nothing but a settlement of karmic accounts . . . Our karmas bring us together and when they are settled, each one goes his own way.

Also from Delusion #12 is this statement:

All these worldly relationships are meant only for clearing our karmic accounts. Different persons who have karmic accounts to settle with us come into our life as our relatives, friends, acquaintances and so forth, and when their accounts are settled they drift away from us. It is our karmas that bring us together and our karmas that separate us from one another. We remain together only as long as we are destined to do so and no more. Sometimes our destiny makes us do things which are much against our wishes. We become a helpless tool in the hands of fate.

Arguably, one reason people may feel a need to believe they have a soul-mate is because of their loneliness, which is actually a natural feeling for all humans. As Saint Charan Singh states in *Quest for Light*:

The deep feeling of loneliness . . . is common and natural to all human beings . . . This constant feeling of loneliness and missing something is in reality the hidden unquenched thirst and craving of the soul for the Lord. It will always persist as long as the soul does not return to its ancient original Home and meet the Lord. Only then will it get true contentment and eternal peace. This feeling has been purposely put in the heart of man. If this natural inclination of the soul towards its Lord had not been there, then perhaps none would have turned to the Creator for solace and peace. It is this feeling that makes us retrace our footsteps from the mad race of living and dying in which we all find ourselves involved.

And here's a legitimate thought. If each of us had a soul-mate, we would most likely be extremely happy, fulfilled, content and satisfied with our life and relationship. There would be no loneliness within us. Our contentment would therefore keep us from searching for something deeper to fill the void, i.e., God. Thus, we could never be divinely free but remain trapped in this nether world.

So rather than lament that we have no soul-mate, no earthly love, we become blessed in that we are forced to search for something else, i.e., for God. Thus, in a very real way it's a good thing there is no such thing as a soul-mate. In Divine Truth, our soul-mate is God, and that will never change. Lucky us.

DELUSION #24

EQUAL POWERS: GOD & SATAN

Forever it seems there has been almost a universal belief that God and Satan are equal powers battling it out in this world. This segment should give millions of people great inspiration, solace and joy because God & Satan having equal powers is nothing more than a grand delusion and perhaps the greatest hoax ever perpetrated on mankind.

In the lexicon of Saints, the word for Satan is Kal. They are one in the same. The names are just a cultural difference and distinction.

First to begin, in speaking of Kal, Guru Nanak simply declares:

Yea, the ruthless Kal is but one morsel of Thine.

In other words Kal, compared to God—the Supreme Being—is nothing except an itty bitty piece of God's domain. Thus, considering Satan/Kal as equal to God is nothing more than a ill-begotten delusion. There is no truth in any of it.

In multiple passages, from *The Master Answers*: Saint Charan Singh explains:

> *Kal is just the administrator of the universe. Kal sees to it that we do not get out of it, that is all . . . He is not without purpose. He is not without the Will of the Lord. He is there through the Will of the Lord. Nothing exists without the Will of the Lord. Kal does not derive his power from anywhere else.*

And . . .

> *The Lord has created the whole world, the Lord has created Kal, and the Lord has given the administration of the whole universe to Kal, that Negative Power, or whatever name you give it.*

And . . .

> *This is all God's creation. In order to run a universe, He needs all sorts of forces to keep people here. If Kal had not been here, we would all have gone back to the Lord again. This universe would not have existed . . . If He does not want this universe, it cannot exist even for a day. It is here because He wants it to be here, and whatever you see, all forces have come from Him.*

And . . .

> *Nothing has come into being without the Father. Nothing existed before creation but the Father . . . So Kal has also come from Him, and he has an allotted task which he is doing.*

And . . .

> *Whatever he [Kal] is doing, he is doing by orders of the Supreme Being.*

Obviously, from the preceding quotes, Kal/Satan is a creation of the Supreme Lord, the Almighty God. There does not exist a rivalry between God and the Devil/Satan/Kal, so the delusion that there is needs to be dissolved. It's nothing more than a trick—this one-on-one battle between two equal Powers. They are not equal at all. God is always in charge and He calls the shots. Satan/Kal is just the administrator of this creation. As Charan Singh says regarding Kal: *He is not without purpose.*

However, we must not be fooled. Kal has a job to do and he's very good at it. Explaining Jesus's viewpoint of Kal from the book *St. John – The Great Mystic,* Saint Charan Singh remarks:

> *Jesus says that Kal, the negative power or Satan, does not want me to show you the path. He does not want a single soul to go beyond his domain. He himself cannot create a soul, nor can he destroy one. All he can do is take an uninitiated soul out of one body and put it in another. But he is just. He rewards or punishes each soul according to the action done by the mind. In this way he determines the destiny and life span of each body and he also decides when and in what form each soul is again to return to this world. The whole cycle of life and death is within his domain, so his one object is to prevent every soul from escaping because only a certain number are allotted to him and he will not get any new ones.*

Saint Sawan Singh says in his book *The Dawn of Light*:

> *The work of Kal is to arrange and maintain this world, and that of the Sant Satguru (the Saint) is to take souls out of it.*

This is the relationship between God and Satan. It is not at all equal. God created the universe and he created Satan to act as a manager of this world and to do as God commands. As Guru Nanak reminds us:

> *Yea, the ruthless Kal is but one morsel of Thine.*

The following passage in the next paragraph is derived from Chapter 8: "The Negative Power" in the book *Messages from the Masters: Timeless Truths for Serious Seekers* (RichardKing.net books & Amazon.com). The speaker is Dr. Julian Johnson— a devout theologian and outstanding surgeon who traveled to India to teach the gospel of Jesus Christ but who, instead, became a devout disciple of the spiritual path of Living Saints. Dr. Johnson is discussing the subject of Kal, the Negative Power, in his landmark book, *The Path of the Masters*.

> *In the meantime, while we sojourn in this dark region of matter, we have to deal with the Negative Power. With him we must contend in our struggles for spiritual freedom. It is his duty to try to hold us here, while it is our duty to try to escape. The resulting struggle purges us and makes us strong, and fits us for our homeward journey. This everlasting fight, this struggle in a welter of pain and blood and heart cries, is designed by the Supreme Father to purge us and make us clean, ready for our homeward ascent. Let us never become discouraged. All of this is designed by the Father for our benefit. It is much as if one enters a gymnasium to take exercise. If we meet these difficulties in the right spirit, we shall greatly profit by*

*them. The idea of pain and struggle is to purge us and inspire in us a
longing to rise above the regions of pain and shadow.*

Thus, we should never equate equal powers to God and Satan, the Kal. They are not equal and any thought of them being so is not only inaccurate, it is pure delusion. Kal has his purpose, as this section has explained, but he was created by the Supreme Power to be a manager of this creation; that's all, and certainly not a god of it.

DELUSION #25

WORLDLY SUCCESS IS GOD'S BLESSING

When we are successful in the world—having riches, fame, fortune, celebrity, notoriety, material goods a plenty, health, wealth, property, beauty, spouse, children, etc.—it is often surmised that such blessings are a gift from God. They may well be, but then again they may well not be.

As we learned in the previous segment, Kal/Satan, who rules this world, *does not want a single soul to go beyond his domain.* So what does this Negative Power do to prevent souls from escaping? After all, his job is to keep people trapped here.

One of the best and most efficient ways to keep human beings imprisoned here is to make sure they have a good life, a successful life, a rich life, a beautiful life. Why? Because if people's lives are pleasant, successful and enjoyable, they won't want to leave. They'll be glued to their comfort in the world and not seek escape from it.

Therefore, worldly success can be a trap, keeping individuals from seeking higher truths, higher understandings of life and creation. Most of all, a successful, enjoyable and fulfilling life here may keep them bound and tied to Kal's domain, ignorant that they actually exist in a prison, a very dark and filthy prison, and that they can actually escape from that prison, i.e., the world, if they are motivated to do so, and return Home to the domain of God, their true Divine residence.

Frankly, when do people normally seek God or answers to their problems, pain, suffering, financial impoverishment and a whole host of other negative circumstances? People seek God when they're hurting and when they need help and comfort. When people have a good life, seldom do they question their life or their so-called blessings.

Therefore, worldly success and other "blessings" may not be blessings at all but snares and traps designed by the Negative Power (Kal/Satan/Devil) to keep people chained to this world and its delusions. Then, because such people never sought God while they were enjoying their success in life, when death comes they end up huge losers and remain prisoners in the forever rotating Wheel of Transmigration which was discussed in Delusion #2—You Only Live Once (Y.O.L.O.).

Is all worldly success a trap of the Negative Power? Of course not, but it is something to consider as we make our way through this world, this incarnation. As long as we're devoted to God and worship Him and His Laws, and do the best we can to place our spiritual well-being above our worldly status and success, we'll be okay. Our devotion, though, must be sincere. God knows if we're faking it or not. Only a purblind fool would try to deceive the Supreme Lord.

Following are some Saints' quotes to corroborate the message of this segment.

The following two quotes are from Saint Charan Singh:

Suffering and pain come to chasten us and are sometimes a blessing in disguise. If there were no pain and suffering in this world, no one would ever turn to God for peace and solace.

Trials and troubles come to us in our life to imprint upon our heart the true nature of the ephemeral pleasures of this world. To a thinking mind these unhappy moments often prove a blessing in disguise.

Baba Jaimal Singh reminds us:

Keep your mind away from worldly desires because you will get only what is written on your forehead. Nothing else. Then why entertain worldly desires and ambitions in the mind?

And . . .

At the end of our life no worldly thing will be of any avail to us.

These quotes tell us that we shouldn't be clamoring for worldly things because our destiny has already been set and we're not going to get anything more or anything less than what has been established for us before we were born.

Furthermore, when we die no worldly thing or success is going with us into the next phase of our existence. So then, why would we spend the whole of our life seeking and acquiring riches, fame, money, celebrity, social status and success when it's all going to be left behind anyway? Yet, sadly, countless numbers of people waste their entire human existence seeking fame and fortune in lieu of seeking God and Soul Liberation. The result is that they lose, big time, in the end and their precious human life was all for naught—indisputably, an irreparable tragic waste.

This is why Saint Kabir remarked:

> *How strange it is that no one seems to care about their future, which is Everlasting Life.*

Sad but true. "Everlasting Life" in this quote does not necessarily equate to a life in paradise, heaven or beyond but rather eternity in the Wheel of Transmigration, being hawked from sub-human form to sub-human form for eons of time, never knowing that there is a God, let alone being able to merge into His Divine Energy.

Exchanging an ephemeral worldly life searching for success and status for an Eternal Life in God's Domain is a bad, bad, bad investment. What could possibly be worse?

Only Saints know the true value of living and following a Divine lifestyle. This is why Saint Tukaram remarks:

> *How can I speak enough of the benefaction of Saints? They are the ones who keep me ever vigilant. How can I repay them for the blessing they bestow? Even the offering of my life is not payment enough.*

In *The Master Answers,* Saint Charan Singh offers these thoughts:

> *Everybody wants peace, but our search for peace is generally in worldly achievements or in worldly possessions. The more we run after these things, the more frustrated and unhappy we are becoming every day.*

Do not become a slave of worldly achievements.

There is no harm in possessing worldly things, but our desire for possessions should not be to that extent that if we do not have them we miss them day and night. That missing creates an attachment within us . . . The possessions in themselves are not harmful. It is our attachment to them or our desire for them that is wrong.

Worldly achievements can never give you permanent happiness.

We have to detach our mind from the senses and the worldly pleasures and attach it to the devotion of the Lord.

From *St. John – The Great Mystic*, Charan Singh advises:

Do not run after worldly possessions. You cannot take them with you and you will even have to leave your own body behind in this world. So make use of the precious gift of the human body by trying to collect that which will help you here and hereafter.

Those who attach themselves to worldly possessions are spiritually dead. They have not found eternal life.

If we are absorbed in devotion to the Lord we are not even interested in the worldly life.

So can we say that worldly success is a blessing from God? No we can't, especially if we're placing God in a subordinate position to worldly success. God first, always and forever. That's the greatest formula for success any human being could ever have.

DELUSION #26

KARMA - REVERSE DELUSION

This work has defined a delusion as a false belief held to be true. A *Reverse Delusion* is a truth held to be false. Karma is a Reverse Delusion. It is indeed true but people, as noted by their everyday actions and behaviors, really think it is false.

Karma is *the* supreme law of this world but why is it a Reverse Delusion? The answer is that if the mass of humanity truly understood karma, they would not be doing many of the things they're doing on a daily basis. In effect they believe karma is false when in actuality it is true.

Karma is based in a very simple principle: we sow, we reap and we cannot reap what we do not sow. In other words, what we put onto the circle of life circles back to encircle us eventually. Yet, most of humanity creates actions every day without thinking that the very actions they're creating— good or bad, positive or negative—will come back to them, but they will. Of this there is no doubt. It's just a matter of time.

The subject of karma is extensively explained in the book, *Karma—The Definitive Guide to the Supreme Law of this World.* (www.RichardKing.net/books & Amazon.com)

As Saint Charan Singh states:

> *Every one, including animals, birds and even plants has its own karmas to go through. The Law of Karma is working relentlessly in this world and all are reaping what they sowed in the past.*

Saint Ravidas remarks:

> *Whatever thou hast sewn, the same shalt thou reap. No change in this shall there ever be and . . . The fruit of action unfailingly overtakes the doer.*

Saint Sawan Singh declares:

> *The law . . . operates without regard to persons.*

He further explains that people who create nefarious, evil and negative actions, although they may not get punished in this life and seem to go scot-free, will ultimately get their just dues and comeuppance.

> *The wicked people, however, suffer heavy punishment for their sins in hell or in their future lives.*

Buddha explains:

> *If you fear pain, if you dislike pain, don't do an evil deed in open or secret. If you're doing or will do an evil deed, you won't escape pain. It will catch you even as you run away.*

Saint Dariya of Bihar announces:

The sower of the poison cannot but be engulfed in the poison.

Saint Charan Singh further explains:

The law of Karma, 'As you sow so shall you reap,' is working relentlessly and we are all reaping what we have sown in the past.

And he emphatically states:

Nothing happens without karma and Karma—nobody can escape, whether one believes it or not.

Saint Dadu explains:

What thou hast not done will never befall thee; only what thou hast done will befall thee.

Saint Sawan Singh shares these realities:

As we sow, so shall we reap. Whatever we are reaping now, we, ourselves, have sown before. Therefore, we are the makers of our own fate.

The Law of Karma is the principal law of the creation: as the action, so is the reward.

The Karmic Law is inexorable and operates without regard to persons.

The Karmic Law is supreme and inevitable and the sooner we reconcile ourselves with it the better.

Saint Jagat Singh weighs in:

> *The Law of Karma is universal. It is the fixed and immutable law of nature. Each soul must reap what it has sown. Every soul shall have to bear the exact consequences of its actions.*

He goes on to say:

> *The Law of Karma is a self-operating law of cause and effect. A seed sown must sprout. Whatever you sow now, you will have to reap either in this birth or the next. Every action produces reaction, which in turn produces further reactions and this vicious circle goes on forever.*

> *Not even a single grain that inadvertently enters your granary from a neighbor's field can go unaccounted. You simply must pay for what you get. The law is inviolable and it cannot be set aside. The payment may be either in kind, in coin, or by transfer of an equivalent good karma, but payment there must be.*

From the Bible we read this:

> *Be not deceived. God is not mocked, for whatsoever a man soweth, that shall he also reap (Galatians 6:7).*

> *Verily I say unto thee, Thou shalt by no means come out thence, till thou hast paid the uttermost farthing (Matthew 5:6).*

The truth of karma is shared by various Saints and Holy Scriptures over and over again to generation after generation, to culture after culture, to wave upon wave of human souls coming and going in this world.

Yet, the great truth of karma and its self-operating reality of sowing and reaping, cause and effect, action and reaction, cause and consequence is shoved aside and ignored as if it never existed in the first place. The following excerpt from *Karma – The Definitive Guide to the Supreme Law of this Creation* may help in understanding this great Law.

THE KARMIC ALGORITHM

The Self-Operating function of karma brings us to the analogy of karma being an algorithm, which is a fitting metaphor for this computer age.

An algorithm is basically an unambiguous, designed, calculation process for solving problems or accomplishing an end. When this creation was designed by its Creator (universally identified as God), an algorithm was developed to govern the creation based on one simple idea:

What we do will be done to us.

Pretty simple, eh? *What we do will be done to us.* This is what is universally known as karma, and it is profound in spite of its simplicity. Karma is the governing algorithm and Law of this world. What we sow, we reap, and we cannot reap what we do not sow. Simple. Simple. Simple. It is not more complicated than that. Yet, this extremely simple idea remains ungrasped by the world at large. It's as if we're living in a blind stupor or in a cave or both, totally ignorant of the very Law that governs every move we make. Blindness could never be more blind.
[end excerpt]

It is hard to comprehend how the Law of Karma—the Supreme Law of this World—could go on being ignored and disclaimed, especially after a cavalcade of Saints, Mystics and Holy teachings have substantiated its veracity. Yet, it has been. Will the world en masse ever catch up to the truth of karma? Who knows, but until that happens karma will remain a Reverse Delusion.

The Karmic Law is supreme and inevitable and the sooner we reconcile ourselves with it the better.

~ Saint Sawan Singh

DELUSION #27

IT'S A
BEAUTIFUL WORLD

From a visual perspective of outer space and the moon, the earth is, indeed, a beautiful world—so blue, white, green and beige. It is stunningly magnificent to look upon.

However, in many ways the world is much like a beautiful and dangerous temptress in the Biblical manner of Bathsheba, Delilah and Jezebel, or in the secular world of Marilyn Monroe, Mata Hari, Greta Garbo and Cleopatra. Their beauty draws you in only to negatively impact or destroy you.

For those people whose lives, loved ones, homes, property and businesses have been destroyed by the earth's tornados, hurricanes, earthquakes, fires, floods, violent winds, storms, droughts and an assortment of lethal disasters, world wars, conflicts and global genocide, the earth is not such a beautiful place at all. Visually, yes, the earth is beautiful. Peacefully, joyfully, ethically, morally, humanitarianly and spiritually, it is not. The earth is definitely not a beautiful place, and from this perspective, the concept of a beautiful world is a delusion.

How can a world, any world, be beautiful when . . .

1. Life lives on death and the daily slaughtering of millions, billions and trillions of living beings simply to fill the stomachs of other living beings? According to animalclock.org on 15 April 2021, the number of animals killed for food in the first 3.5 months of this year is 15,680,248,424 or in words: fifteen billion, six hundred eighty million, two hundred forty-eight thousand, four hundred twenty-four. And this is just in the United States! What of other countries in the world? What about killings in the animal kingdom, oceanic kingdom, aviary kingdom and insect kingdom? The whole of life on planet earth exists on killing. How is this beautiful? It's not, which is why Saints recommend a vegetarian diet. Yes, plants are killed to feed other living beings but it's easier to pay off the karma of killing plants than killing higher forms of life.

2. The world is full of hatred on personal, public and global scales. Hate is neither a beautiful or loving energy. It is, frankly, demonic. How can the world be beautiful when saturated with hate?

3. From time to time the world experiences pandemics and plagues. How are these beautiful?

4. In 2021 the population of the world is close to eight billion. Millions of people on planet earth live under the dictatorship of tyrants. How is being enslaved a condition of beauty? Freedom is beautiful. It dwells in the heart of every human, but its full and complete manifestation does not exist on planet earth. How is enslavement beautiful?

5. Tragically, the world of sports and various corporations throughout the world support the enslavement of countries and dictators who create

a state of enslavement. All of this is done in the quest of money. Such a sickness is never beautiful.

6. The world's consumption of recreational drugs and alcohol—substances which damage and destroy life—continues to increase. Beautiful? Hardly.

7. Then there are the thieves, heartless souls who scam others and steal their money, identification, property, etc. This kind of behavior is really ugly.

8. What about abortions? Killing babies in the womb is really an act of detestable ugliness. And what about selling baby body parts? This is so vile it hurts to even think about such dark conduct. Woe be unto the souls engaged in this demonic behavior. The karmic payback of such acts will be horrendous.

9. As of this writing, nine countries possess nuclear weapons which could easily destroy the entire world if a global conflagration were to erupt. Those nine countries are Russia, the United States, France, China, the United Kingdom, Pakistan, India, Israel and North Korea. How is it beautiful having to live under the potential threat of a nuclear holocaust?

10. Although strikingly beautiful against the black background of space, the earth is vulnerable to its own internal calamities, such as the shifting of its tectonic plates, volcanic eruptions, geomagnetic reversals, as well as civilization-ending asteroid impacts.

11. Then there are what Saints refer to as the five hindrances, five passions, five poisons and five perversions which plague every human on the earth. These five poisons are pride, anger, greed, attachment and lust. Just stop and think how many problems every second of every day around the world are generated by any one of these five hindrances. Such conduct is definitely not beautiful.

We could continue ad-infinitum about how this world, aside from its physical beauty, is not beautiful at all. When we stop and think about it even for a few seconds, we realize how ugly and sick this world really is. This isn't being negative. It's being realistic and honest.

Saints do not think highly of this world at all. Quite the opposite. Saint Charan Singh is very definitive about what this world is and how we should deal with it. He says:

> This whole world is a dark and filthy dungeon . . . You do not belong to this world . . . Just live in the world and get out of it.

By "get out" he means to rise spiritually into higher realms of love and light via the purification of our soul. Of this world, Saint Charan Singh advises:

> All efforts should be made to get out of this realm of the Prince of Darkness as quickly as possible.

How much more direct can a Saint be? If this were a beautiful world full of love and light, peace and harmony, no Saint would admonish us to leave. But it's not a beautiful world. It's a dark world, an ugly world, a world to escape from not to live in.

Kabir states:

> The world is blind, engulfed in utter darkness, but to whom can I explain this?

And . . .

> Among all that are born of flesh, remember, none is happy;
> All those you see are miserable.

Ravidas points out:

> *The world is a house of collyrium [an abode of evil]; a veritable well of the poison of egotism.*

Mira Bai exclaims:

> *This world is truly a cauldron of evil.*

Tukaram remarks:

> *This world is a destroyer of the self. It only separates him from the Lord.*

Saint Dariya of Bihar observes:

> *This world indeed is an ocean of miseries . . . a sea of sorrow. The world has indeed turned insane.*

Swami Ji shares these truths:

> *There is utter chaos in this world . . . The world is engulfed in the darkness of ignorance . . . This world, which is a wilderness has been mistaken for a residence.*

Baba Ji Maharaj admonishes us:

> *Always keep this idea firmly in your mind: we do not belong to this world.*

Saint Sawan Singh notes:

> *This world is the plane of struggle . . . The sins of the world are mounting . . . This world is the lowest and most miserable of all . . . There is no peace in this world . . . The thing for us to do is to get to the Light ourselves as fast as possible.*

Saint Jagat Singh declares:

> *The world is literally a Pandora's Box—a home of misfortune. Quit this place as soon as possible . . . This world is full of gloom and misery. None here is happy.*

Given this description of the delusion as to why the world is not beautiful, except for its scenery, may tend to create in us a level of negativity. However, there is an extremely bright side to all this. After all, everything in this dimension has two sides: one positive, one negative. We've discussed the negative, so how about the positive?

Truth is always beautiful. It may be hard to swallow when we are first made aware of it but let's face it: Would we rather live in delusion or truth? Truth may hurt but it will never destroy or impede and can, in fact, liberate us.

This book has shared twenty-seven delusions which plague mankind. When we realize the untruths of such delusions, we can expand our consciousness of Reality and benefit from its truths. This is what Saints do—they tell us the Truth of life on this earth and let us deal with it. They don't sugar coat it. They don't falsify it. They don't tell us lies to make us feel good. They don't deal in delusions or deceit. They don't mislead us in any way. They always tell us what we need to hear so we can make spiritual progress while in our precious human form and eventually escape from this extremely miserable world and climb to higher worlds, higher realities, higher realms of radiant light and truly loving vibrations. In effect, Saints come to detach us from this nether land and return us to our true Home.

[end of the 27 Delusions]

FINAL NOTE:

If you have an interest in the teachings and writings of Saints, you can find information at the following two links:

1. RSSB.org (stands for Radha Soami Satsang Beas)

2. ScienceOfTheSoul.org

There you will find many books by various Saints in multiple languages—all exist in service to your Divine Being and spiritual success.

So . . . here's to dissolving the delusions that chain and enslave us to this dark world and impede, even negate, our spiritual progress. May you destroy these malefic delusions and live life fully aware of what is true and what is not, of what continues to bind you to this world or what helps you in transcending it. Best wishes in your Divine Ascent. God Speed!

RICHARD ANDREW KING - BOOKS

RichardKing.net/books & Amazon.com

The King's Book of Numerology Series (KBNS)

1. *The King's Book of Numerology: Volume I – Foundations & Fundamentals*

2. *The King's Book of Numerology 2 (II): Forecasting – Part 1*

3. *The King's Book of Numerology 3: Master Numbers*

4. *The King's Book of Numerology 4: Intermediate Principles*

5. *The King's Book of Numerology 5: IR Sets – Level 1*

6. *The King's Book of Numerology 6: Love Relationships*

7. *The King's Book of Numerology 7: Parenting Wisdom – Numerology & Life Truths*

8. *The King's Book of Numerology 8: Forecasting – Part 2*

9. *The King's Book of Numerology 9: Numeric Biography, Princess Diana*

10. *The King's Book of Numerology 10: Historic Icons – Part 1*

11. *The King's Book of Numerology 11: The Age of the Female – Volumes 1 & 2*

12: *The King's Book of Numerology 12: Advanced Principles*

Numerology books published separately

The Age of the Female – A Thousand Years of Yin (KBN11)

Your Love Numbers – Discovering The Secrets of Your Life, Loves & Relationships (KBN6)

Destinies of the Rich & Famous – The Secret Numbers of Extraordinary Lives (KBN10)

Parenting Wisdom for the 21st Century – Raising Your Children By Their Numbers To Achieve Their Highest Potential (KBN7)

Blueprint of a Princess – Diana Frances Spencer, Queen of Hearts (KBN9)

Non-Numerology books

Karma-The Definitive Guide to the Supreme Law of this World

Messages from the Masters – Timeless Truths for Spiritual Seekers

The Black Belt Book of Life – Secrets of a Martial Arts Master

The Karate Consciousness – From Worldly Warrior to Mystic Master

Parenting Wisdom – What to Teach the Children (Part 2 of KBN7)

The Age of the Female II – Heroines of the Shift (Part 2 of KBN11)

The Galactic Transcripts

99 Poems of the Spirit

27 Delusions of Mankind

ORDER INFORMATION

To order Books go to
RichardKing.net, Amazon.com
or major online retailers

CONTACT

Richard Andrew King
PO Box 3621
Laguna Hills, CA 92654
RichardKing.net
Rich @ RichardKing.net

160

NOTES:

NOTES:

NOTES:

NOTES:

164

NOTES:

NOTES:

166

NOTES:

NOTES:

168

NOTES:

www.ingramcontent.com/pod-product-compliance
Lightning Source LLC
Chambersburg PA
CBHW021232090426
42740CB00006B/502